WHY GOD BIRTHED AMERICA

God's Purpose For Men and Nations

SIXTH PRINTING

Don Pinson

WHY GOD BIRTHED AMERICA

God's Purpose For Men and Nations

Don Pinson

PUBLISHED BY:
BRENTWOOD CHRISTIAN PRESS
WWW.BRENTWOODBOOKS.COM
1-800-334-8861

CONTENTS

FOREWORD

by Dr. Paul Jehle

I have known Don Pinson of Kentucky for more than two decades now. In some ways, he is a pioneer, and in others, he is a patriot. When you read this book, I think you will agree. Many years ago, Daniel Boone cut a path through the wilderness of Kentucky. Committed to principles of liberty and justice based upon the laws of God, Boone is known as a true patriot and pioneer. In fact, he was cutting a path through the wilderness at the same time the patriots were standing firm on Lexington Green. The liberty that was won in the American Revolution was destined by the Providence of God to spread through the paths that had once been a wilderness. So it must be again today.

Don has taken time to do his homework and study the roots of our nation. He has traveled to New England, Washington DC and other places on the East Coast where our history has taken place. In a sense, he has studied the paths already cut in the wilderness at the time of America's founding and retold them for you. As a true patriot, he teaches seminars and conducts tours in a plain style anyone can understand. In essence, this readable book will inspire you to carry the principles of liberty drawn from the Bible and initially protected by our Constitution. You will be asked to travel the once well-worn paths that are now covered with the wilderness of weeds and neglect.

Don has now traveled from one end of Kentucky to the other. What's more, he did it with his wife, Vickie, and their children, Joel and Christis. He has demonstrated that restoration must begin at home, but has also illustrated that it must not end there. In his very readable style, Don will take you on a journey from Creation to the Cross, and then from the Reformation to the birth of America. Most importantly, you won't just learn *how* America was born, but you will learn *why*. God has a purpose for everything that He performs. Nothing happens by accident. As you read this book, you will get a sense that you are not reading it by accident either.

The same God that birthed America is at work to restore her paths through the wilderness that has grown due to neglect as well as deliberate attack. Are you ready? Will you pick up your axe and begin to clear the brush? When you learn *why* God birthed our beloved America, you may also learn *why* God birthed you. Every American needs to find their destiny and purpose, and what better place to do so then by the retelling of the once familiar story every child in America knew at one time. My friend, the God of America is also the God of the individual, for it is there that He decreed that all liberty should be birthed. It is there, in the heart of the individual, that self-government was to begin.

Let the God of the Bible inspire you to join the millions of others who are rebuilding the waste places and restoring our nation one individual at a time. May you find your purpose in Jesus Christ, expressing the law of liberty, and committing yourself to the task of seeing our nation, once again, become; *"one nation under God."*

Dr. Paul Jehle
Cedarville, Mass.
March 2009

Acknowledgements:

To Vickie, my faithful wife of 35 years.
Always the one who prays most for me. Always the one who believes I can do more and better than I think I can; I say, "Thank you for always being there as my "helpmeet"! I love you!

To Joel and Christis Joy, our son and daughter;
For praying for Dad, and giving _invaluable_ suggestions and wonderful words of encouragement. And like your Mother, giving me up to my 'cave of writing' in order to finish this work; I say, "Thanks so much! I love you and I'm very proud of you both!"

To Mrs. Pauline Pinson, my Mother;
For you and Dad laying the foundational ideas in me that prepared me to receive the truths expressed in this book. "Thanks Mom for all your patience and most of all your prayers!"

To Mrs. Janice Johnson, my sister;
For reading the manuscript and encouraging me with your kind words. Thanks for the effort in the midst of an overwhelming schedule!

To Dr. Paul Jehle, my good friend and mentor;
For teaching me so much concerning America's history and government. Whatever I know of America's original systems of education, economy and government, you are the source for the better part of that knowledge: For taking time from an already overloaded schedule to read and re-read the manuscript, and for your inestimable work of making sure this work was historically accurate: For writing the Forward and

helping to make possible the publishing of this book, I offer my warmest thanks and sincere gratitude!

To "Di Di" Hallman;
For your tremendous effort in correcting the script grammatically: I am in your debt for adding this to your already existing overload of tasks to complete at this time. I sincerely believe your effort has improved the communication of the text to such an extent that many people will be blessed who otherwise would have missed much of the book's message. I do believe God will reward you richly for your persistent effort. Thank you so very much!

To Mrs. Tonya Mooreland:
The best 5th grade public school teacher I know. You and Dave are great friends and tremendous co-workers! For reading and re-reading the manuscript and offering your very helpful suggestions concerning grammar, chapter titles, and a host of other things, I say, "Thank you so very much!"

To Mr. Todd Hopper;
For your very encouraging words after reading the manuscript: It helped me believe we were accomplishing the reason for writing it. Likewise thanks for your other help in copyrighting the book.

To other special friends who have taken of your time to read the manuscript and offer your very helpful suggestions, I say a special "Thanks": Namely, Dr. James Castlin, Colonel Steve Robinson, Rev. Gary Stommel, Dr. and Mrs. Stephen Anderson, Shirley Pinson, and Michelle Hannah.

May the combined effort of all these precious family and friends, along with my own, prove to be the work of 'Christ in us, the hope of glory!' (Colossians 1:27)

Don Pinson, September, 21, 2008

Introduction

The idea for this book has been in my heart for many years. I first had revealed to me the Biblical truths, which are the foundation for it, over thirty years ago. They have become the most precious truths of my life.

Having come through a time of personal crisis and subsequent deeper surrender to Christ in January, 1972, I found the Bible to be a "new" Book to me. It seemed everywhere I read, God was saying something to me that met my most pressing needs. It was during these months that I began to read the Bible completely through, which I now make a yearly practice. I began to get an overview of His plan for man that would revolutionize my thinking about His reasons for creating mankind. I've never been the same since.

Some ten years after that, He began to bring to my attention stories and quotes of America's Founding Fathers. I was astounded as to the Christian philosophy they lived and expressed with their words. Majoring in college (at two so-called "Christian" schools) in both History and Political Science, I had never *once* heard of the deep faith in Christ that now I was finding nearly every time I read their own writings. I wondered why.

The more I researched, the more I began to realize that their Christian legacy had been purposely stolen from us. It both greatly angered and deeply grieved me to think that the source of greatest inspiration and wisdom in America's long history was, by design, being hidden from each new generation. I wanted to do something to restore this precious information. But the Lord wasn't ready.

It's interesting how God insists that we walk out His principles before we teach them. The record of Jesus' life on earth reveals this principle. He teaches in Matthew 5:19 that we must "do" before we "teach." He wanted me to *walk* more in what they knew before He would entrust to me the *teaching* of it. While I yet feel woefully inadequate, I have been deeply burdened that now is, indeed, His time to communicate what He's shown me about *why He birthed America*. Hence the title of this book.

However, a few statements are in order to explain the style and format of this work:

This book is not written to impress so-called scholars who have set themselves against the Bible as absolute truth. This is a book written for the common person. I've attempted, as much as was possible, to write in the common language of the people of America. I haven't the slightest interest in impressing the "edu-crats" of the elitist crowd who work to change America to atheism and socialism. If I know my heart, I could not care *less* what they think!

The people I do hope will be influenced by it are the ones who get up and go to work every day at their own businesses, or as someone's employees. The person I hope to communicate with is the one who loves his or her spouse and children: The one who cares about his neighbor and seeks to "do unto others as you would have them do unto you." I desire to influence those "salt-of-the-earth" people who do the "living and the dying" in this nation, and who are wise enough to know that they aren't the ones with the final answer: They know they need an outside source of Truth to compare their ideas to, and they go to the Bible for that. My hope is that the "honest-hearted" individual will read this and determine that he will research the Bible and the writings of America's Founders to see if there *was* a link between God's general plan for mankind and the birthing of America. *These are the real Americans!*

Because, I want the common man to read and understand it, I've attempted to make it a relatively short book. The average American's lifestyle is already much too busy. My prayer is that this can be read in a few hours and, without being overwhelming, impart life-changing truths about the purpose of God for man, as well as the American nation in particular. Though the title of the book refers to the birthing of America, the reader will notice how the first half of the book is given to explaining what God did in creating and redeeming man. This is a purposeful attempt to help us regain the understanding that all events on this earth have their roots in the overall purpose of God. It is the author's humble effort to restore the truth that all things in this natural realm are first birthed in the spiritual realm. Hopefully, the reader will come to see that America, or any other nation, has no specific purpose apart from the over-all purpose of God for man.

It is with this simple desire, along with a prayer that God will use this in your life to His intended glory, that I share with you: *Why God Birthed America*.

Don Pinson, Clay County, Kentucky January 13, 2007

Chapter 1

Why God Made Man

Jesus has been hanging for six hours on a rough, Roman cross. His body is wracked with pain, His mind oppressed by forces both natural and spiritual. He knows the end of His earthly life is near.

Suddenly, with a cry of triumph, He lifts His voice and declares, "It is finished!" The air resounds with the declaration! There's a finality about it. All creation is suddenly arrested with the awareness that a most important work is now completed.

"It is finished," He had said. What was finished? What work was now completed? What potent meaning lies just beneath the surface of the words, "It is finished?"

The clause "It is finished," in the Greek language, in which Jesus spoke it, means to reach a goal. It also means to pay a debt in full, so that the books balance. Jesus had reached His goal of paying our debt. Perhaps you're thinking: "What debt?" – I'm glad you want to know.

To understand the "debt" Jesus was paying, we must revisit the scene in the Garden of Eden when God begins to work with a pile of dust: He carefully shapes it into the form of a man. Perhaps the animals gather around to watch, sensing the Creator is doing something new and wonderful.

Once the human body is finished to perfection, God "blows" His own breath into the nostrils of this pile of clay. All of a sudden, the shaped form moves! Light comes to its eyes! It gets up and stands erect, like God. I can see Father God turning to the rest of His creation and saying, "This is man. He is made in Our image, after Our likeness, to have dominion over all creation."[1] At that point every animal, plant, and element bowed in submission to their newly appointed ruler.

Here was man–made in the likeness of the Creator God. He was the very image of God: Father, Son, and Holy Spirit. He is endowed with earth's highest form of existence. He is made in the "image and likeness" of God–capable of looking, living, and ruling like God.[1] God has literally made him to be an expression of His life: A vessel God can come to dwell in, and through which He can express *Himself* to the world.

Man, who God calls (in our language) *Adam*, is not created as a separate entity with a destiny separate from that of his Creator. He is literally a mobile house; a place in which God can dwell on this earth. He is a channel through which God can flow to all creation. Man is not his own. His life is a *stewardship gift* from the Creator. Adam's life was not his own to be used for whatever he wanted. His existence on this earth was to be a distribution point from which God's life could flow to the world. This is why Paul, the Apostle, would later state that man's very being was wrapped up in the life of His Creator.[2] As the Bible declares, Man was "not his own."[3]

Think of the potential: Adam had the possibility of being a dwelling place for his Creator! God, the Almighty, wanted to take up residence inside of Adam. He wanted to fill his mind with His mind. He wanted to fill his will with His will. He wanted to fill his emotions with His feelings. Man had the opportunity to be the channel through which God could flow to the world. He could be the pipeline which would allow the vibrant life of God to be delivered to all creation.

Think what this could mean to Adam's sons and daughters. Through their father (and mother, whom God would soon create), they would be able to receive the life of God and, in turn, become a channel through which their own children could receive that Life. Their children would not experience God through some 'osmosis' process, though. Rather, it would be the natural result of God speaking His truth to them through their parents. Likewise, because God would be living inside their parents' souls and bodies, He would be able to demonstrate through those parents how He could live out the truth He was teaching them. Thus, the next generation would receive both the "form" and the "Spirit" of God's original purpose for man. Their potential was astounding!

But God has never been into making robots. He wanted man to choose Him to be his life. He wanted a relationship with man in which man made the choice to allow God to come inside of him and express His life through him.

This was the reason for the two trees. God placed two trees in the Garden for the purpose of allowing man a choice as to whether he would receive the life of God as that which would indwell him–be his energy, his life. He would not force his way into our hearts, raping and wounding us so as to prevent our being able to return His love. He would woo us by showing us Himself. He came to walk with Adam daily in the garden, so mankind could learn how He thinks. In those times of sharing, God revealed His mind to Adam–listened to Adam's heart. It was designed, in time, to bring Adam to think as God Himself thinks. Thus, a covenant (which means "a meeting or agreement of minds"[4]) could be established between them, and God would begin to flow through Adam to all creation.

This is what the Tree of Life[5] represented. Since God is life,[6] the Tree of Life represented a way of life in which God is the Source. The fruit hanging on the Tree of Life was an open, physical way man could say to God (before all creation), "I receive Your life as my life. You can come to live inside me and express Your life through me. My spirit can be the home of Your Spirit. My soul (my will, mind, and emotions) can be the home of Your thinking processes, Your decision-making, and Your feelings. My life can be a three-room house (spirit, soul, and body) that You can dwell in, and through which You can express Yourself."

Had man chosen to eat the fruit of the Tree of Life, he would have known the ultimate fulfillment. He would have come to know his Creator in the most intimate way possible. The mind of God would have been so interspersed throughout the mind of man, it would have been impossible to tell the two apart. His thinking would have produced decisions through which the will of God could flow. The will of God flowing through him would have affected his feelings and the actions of his body. When others saw him, they would have immediately recognized the character of the Creator. He would have become a mobile house God could move in all over the earth. He would be the image of God. He would express the actions of God. He would be ruling on earth like God rules over heaven and earth. Man would be completely fulfilled because he would be walking in the purpose for which he was created.

But alas, it was not to be–not yet.

There was another Tree in that Paradise: The Tree of the Knowledge of Good and Evil[7]. This tree represented the opposite way of life. This way of living would be motivated by what happened outside of man. Instead of being inspired by the moving of the Life of God deep within him, if he chose to eat of this tree, he would be rejecting God's offer to come inside of him and be his life. He would be choosing a way in which he would make his own decisions, instead of allowing the flowing will of God to come through him.

Consider the name of this tree. It was the *Tree of the Knowledge of Good and Evil*. The Hebrew word for *knowledge* comes from a root word which, in essence, means to know by experience.[8] If Adam ate of this tree, he would be saying to God: "God, I want to experience the good, and I want to experience the evil in a particular situation, and I want to make my own decision as to which I think is best for me." He would be saying, "I want to decide what's best for me. I know better than You what direction my life should go." He would be declaring his independence from God. Instead of looking like God, he would begin to look (much of the time) like satan in whose steps he would be following. Instead of being an expression of the life of God, he would be an expression of selfishness–the attitude which says, "I want what I want when I want it." Instead of being a house God could dwell in, he would be opening himself up to other "tenants." Stated simply: He would be saying I want to make my own decisions.

Tragedy of all tragedies, Adam chose to go his own way. He ate of the Tree of the Knowledge of Good and Evil. Notwithstanding that he was helped along in this decision by the master of deceit (satan himself), Adam was still responsible for his decision. The best word to describe his action is – sin. The word *sin* means to "miss the mark." God had a plan for man to be a vessel through which His own life could flow. Man "missed that mark." The stewardship of life God had entrusted to us was now marred. We had taken a gift and used it as if we owned it. We had stolen a perfect life and filled it with imperfection. We had treated as worthless the greatest gift God had given to us–the gift of life. Now, *that* life is contaminated with the "sin principle."

This root of selfishness now spread like gangrene and attached itself to every part of man–spirit, soul, and body. The fruit of selfishness, which is death, began to eat away at man's whole being. He who was created in the very image of God now is permeated with rebellion against his Creator. He has stolen a life which God entrusted to him to be used as a vessel for the flow of His own life. Mankind now owes God a debt–*one perfect life*.

The trouble is, man no longer has a perfect life which he can bring to God to pay his debt. His life, now being filled with rebellion, is no longer perfect. It cannot be used as currency with which to pay his debt. And because Adam would pass that sin on to the next generation (and they to their children), no child of Adam was ever capable of paying the debt. Mankind was hopelessly indebted to God with no hope of avoiding the consequence of death–both physical and spiritual death. Man was bankrupt!

What now? Is the noble dream of man being a vessel God could flow through lost forever? Is all possibility of man intimately knowing his Creator gone for eternity? Is man hopelessly lost?

Well, yes–and no!

Let me explain.

Chapter 2

God Shows Us What's Right–And What's Wrong!

Looking at man's situation from the human perspective he is hopelessly lost. He is filled with the selfish attitude of, "I want what I want when I want it," no one could pay man's debt of one perfect life which was owed to God; no one would be able to break the cycle and come up with a perfect life. Thus, from man's viewpoint, there was no hope!

"But God"[1] – Because He still *is*, let's not make the mistake of looking at man's state from man's perspective. Ultimately, we're not dealing with man here; we're dealing with God. This is God Almighty! This is the Creator God! This is the infinitely wise God. This is the God Who always triumphs! This is the God Who never gives up on His dream! This is "the Eternal 'Isness'."[2] This God <u>always finishes what He starts!</u>

So how does God go about finishing what He started?

God starts this restoration process by tapping a shepherd on the shoulder. Moses by name, this man's attention is arrested by a bush that burns but is not banished. As he investigates this mystery, God calls to him from the bush and commissions him to go into Egypt and bring out the enslaved descendants of Abraham, his forefather. After overcoming Moses' pleas of inability (no small task), He tells him to bring these millions out into the desert: He wants to have a heart to heart talk with them. And, though these people want deliverance from their hard bondage to Pharoah, most of them have little remembrance of this God of their fathers. Even though God called Abraham for the very purpose of his teaching his children Who God was and what His plan for them was, his descendents had not continued to teach the next generation.[3] Some of this present generation are now so skeptical they have little respect for the agreement Abraham, and his son Issac, and his son Jacob (Israel), had made with God several generations ago.

But God doesn't have the short memory we do. He still respects their agreement (called a "covenant") and intends to carry out His end of the bargain. He intends to use this nation to get His "light" back into the world. And provided they are *willing* to be used by Him, He plans to reward them beyond their greatest imagination.[4] He's had a privileged plan for man all along to be a vessel of His life. *He is going to accomplish His plan!*

However, the more immediate problem is that mankind has forgotten that God thinks this way. In fact, man has forgotten most of what God thinks–about most things! In the beginning God had taught the early generations on the earth that the fathers were to teach their children Who He was.[5] But with the sin principle at work in man, he often got distracted (sometimes for a lifetime) and simply didn't do this all-important task. Thus, as time went on, ignorance grew and the knowledge of Who the Creator was and how He thought was mostly lost.

But now, God has in mind to reveal His mind to man in such a way *he won't ever forget it.*

By miracles, He brings Abraham's children to the desert mountain known as Sinai. Here He calls Moses up on the mountain and shows Himself in ways never yet experienced by man. In an awesome display of thunder, lightning, and the quaking of this huge mountain, God shows these "children of Israel" that He is the God who created them and is worthy of their utmost respect.

To begin this "mind altering" process in man, God brings an overwhelmed Moses up on this mountain, and with His torch-like Hand, begins to engrave letters into the rock. Moses watches in awe as ten commands are burned into the side of Sinai. God then, with His finger, cuts the outline of two tablets, separating them from the rest of the rock bed. Moses watches the smoking tablets, completely enraptured with the momentous thing he's just viewed. He then begins to read the writing on the tablets: "You shall have no other gods before me...": Ten such commands revealing how God thinks about Himself, about man, and how he expects us to treat Him and those He's created. Moses hears God telling him he's to take these to the people at the foot of the mountain. God wants men to know how he thinks; and because He wants them not to forget it, *He's written it down.*

The effect of this Sinai experience will be world-changing. Now, for the first time, the mind of God has been summarized and written in stone. Anytime man reads these words he is gripped by the challenge of them. These noble ideals inspire him to "reach for the stars," to be all he was created to be. He longs to walk in these precepts: *But he can't.*

Though he is stirred to his depths in wanting to obey these commands, and though he tries with the best he has in him, he simply cannot obey these commands indefinitely. There is something inside him that will not let him walk these out. It's difficult to describe, but he finds that when he wants to obey these good laws, evil is always present;[6] and at least some of the time he yields to this evil, which resists the rulership of God. Try as he might, he simply cannot carry out these ten commands without failing at least part of the time. It almost seems to him as if they were designed to keep him from obeying.

While it's *not* true that God built these commands with an inherent power to make man disobey, it *is* true that they were given to reveal to man the deeply rooted selfishness which now controlled him. They were put together for the purpose of making man see that he had fallen from the position he originally had with God.[7] The commands were to open up to man the depravity deep within him that kept him from being a vessel through which God could express Himself. This would create a sense of desperation that would cause us to admit we were not fulfilling our destiny. This desperation was designed to stir us to look for a deliverer: Someone Who could forgive our failures and Who could restore us to what God intended us to be. And that is precisely why God gave them! As the Bible states it: "The law is become our tutor to bring us to Christ."[8]

Every experience of man from Moses to Jesus was designed to show us we could not possibly be what God had created us to be without this Deliverer. We needed someone to both pay our debt to the Father (the one perfect life we'd stolen in the Garden), and to deliver us from the "old man" (the mixture of our bodily desires with the selfishness now resident within us).

This brings us to the center point of history. By the way, history really is just "His Story!" "His Story" likewise includes the birthing of America. We're about to see His *reason* for everything He's done in this earth–including creating America. The most important part of God's whole plan is about to be revealed.

Chapter 3

God Invades Human Flesh

The unveiling of this centerpiece begins in an obscure village in Palestine called Nazareth. An unknown young maiden is startled one day by a visit from an angel who identifies himself as being no less than Gabriel himself. He tells Mary (for that was her name), that she will have a child–though she is a virgin–and that this child will be called "the Son of the Most High."[1] It was further revealed to her perplexed fiancé, Joseph, that "She shall bear a son, and you shall call his name Jesus, because He will save His people from their sins."[2] Mary is shocked! *She*–bear the long-awaited "Anointed One?" *She* was to give birth to the One Who would pay man's debt to God? *She* was to bring into this world the One Who would fix what we had messed up in the Garden of Eden? This seemed incredible! Yet, the credibility of this mighty angel standing before her is hardly debatable.

And then the realization hits her! She is a virgin. How can she possibly bear a child? She looks at the angel with her puzzled look and asks, "How can this be, seeing I know not a man?" The question was honest and sincere. It wasn't an accusation against God's ability. It was merely a desire to know what sort of operation God was going to use to bring this about. Gabriel candidly informed her that the Holy Spirit would plant the child in her womb. Mary simply believed what he told her, not doubting the ability of God to bring it about.

Some nine months later, the most unique child ever birthed entered into this world. He was uniquely God and uniquely man. He was Son of God and Son of man. Yet this was the plan of God for restoring mankind to Himself. This unique birth made possible the paying of our "sin-debt" as well as the deliverance from bondage to self and satan.

His name was called Jesus, as God had related to Mary and then later to her husband, Joseph. The name means "Deliverer." This was indeed Who He would be. He would give us a new vision of hope by the very way He lived. He would actually cast an example for us by *doing* the things God has always intended man to do. He would look like God in this world. He would live like God in this world. He would rule like God in this world. *His life would show what man's life would have been like had we chosen to eat of the Tree of Life and receive the life of God, instead of choosing to make our own decisions based on our experience.*

You couldn't meet Him without being affected. All who felt His gaze knew He was different. He would look into the eyes of fishermen and simply state, "Follow me," and they would choose to leave their family and their livelihood to follow Him around the countryside. He would look into the eyes of Nicodemus and reveal to him that a 'new birth' was the process by which we could come to know God. He would look into the eyes of Zacchaeus, go home with him–and deliver him from the greed that had controlled his life. He would look into the eyes of a woman caught in the act of adultery, and she would see mercy and help. Once their eyes met His, they knew they had met a "different" One. They had seen God in a human body, simply looking, thinking, and acting the way *He does all the time.*

Yet He was unmistakenly *a man.* He had to eat, rest, and sleep just like all other men. He laughed and wept just as all humans have since the dawn of creation. He had to manage money and relate to relatives. Yet the peace and confidence with which He did it all was amazing. It was as if He wasn't weighted down as they were. He talked about His Father and His Spirit in such a familiar way that They seemed close, not far off in an unreachable heaven. His followers would later come to recognize this uniqueness as the very fulfillment of what God intended man to be all along. In short, *they would come to know they had seen God's presence living in a human body.*[3]

But as Jesus brought God near to man, He revealed *differences* in *our* thinking and *God's* thinking. Though He taught a great deal about money, it never seemed to occupy the center of His thoughts the way it does most human beings. At times He had multitudes swarming around Him; and while He seemed to always have time for others, you got the impression His greatest desire was to be alone with His Father. And when the crowd came to make Him king, He almost seemed to ignore their request, making it plain He wasn't interested in the prestige (or responsibility) they desired to heap on Him. And though He noticed the beauty of woman, He never gave into the temptation to lust or experience her body. He seemed to have His eyes fixed on another goal.[4]

That focus defined His life. Everything He did was directed at fulfilling the vision for His life, which the Father had released in His heart. This desire to obey the Father in order to bring men back to God consumed Him. Though He went through everything we do that can so easily distract us from our goal, He constantly looked to the Father in order to interpret present circumstances in the light of the vision–in order not to allow them to take captive His focus. He was "living in the light of eternity." What happened here had significance only if it helped to reach the goal of His Father for eternity. He was not living for Himself: He acknowledged His life was not His own. As a man, it wasn't about Him; it was about the Father's desire being realized. His human life was designed as a vessel the Father's life could flow through–the Spirit of God released in the life of a man. *God's original purpose for man was now being shown in perfect form.*

When asked by His followers to reveal the Father to them, He simply stated, "He who has seen Me has seen the Father . . . Do you not believe that I am in the Father, and the Father in Me? The words that I speak to you I do not speak on My own authority, but the Father who dwells in Me does the works."[5] Watching Jesus was like having a front row seat in the Throne room of God; you were constantly seeing the Father in action.

Yet, this "Throne room experience" came to a puzzling end. Though for months Jesus had been trying to tell His followers what lay just ahead, they just couldn't seem to grasp it. The whirlwind of activity and acceptance by the multitudes was intoxicating. It left little time (or, for that matter, *desire*) to reflect on the deeper meaning of the mission of Christ. Like so many of us, they were living for the *moment*. And what a *moment* it was! They had never seen such amazing things! Nor had they ever had this much *respect from people*. Their association with Jesus had made them highly visible and envied by the common folk. They were "on a roll!"

But Jesus had not come to cater to our selfish desires. He would not play the world's game of trying to build our own self-image by gaining the acceptance of others, neither would He allow His followers to do it. He must bring them to the awakening of who they *really* were–of *why they* were here on this earth. That realization would not come through the recognition or rewards of the world system. All of this "acceptance" would shortly meet an abrupt end.

Jesus' disciples were vaguely aware of the growing anger toward Him by the people in authority. Both the religious and civil leaders were afraid of the acceptance the common people had given Him. *Nothing is so feared by tyrants as a growing ideal among the masses.* Jesus had been teaching the common folk why they were alive, and they had "come alive" in response to His message. The authorities feared an open revolt, which would spell the end of their power and position–and the wealth associated with it. Thus, (as always with demagogues) they decided it would be best dealt with using death–death to the One Who this 'movement' (as they perceived it) was centered around. Their verdict: Jesus must die. As Caiaphas, the high priest said it, "One should die for the people."[6]

Thus, the framework for Jesus to show His followers the greatest reason He came to this earth was now in place. After Jesus spent the evening with His closest followers in an upstairs room, summing up for them His mission and their part in it, He proceeded to a favorite place of His. It was a quiet grove of olive trees–a place where He often came to meet with His Father. This night, though, was the most difficult He would ever spend within these trees.

As He entered this grove, He asked His followers to use their time praying with and for Him. They certainly cared for Him and could tell He was very burdened about something. And though He had stated it quite plainly early in the evening, they seemed dull and unable to receive the message of His, soon-to-be, suffering and death. Thus, though they tried to pray for a while, sleep quickly overtook them; and Jesus was left to fight alone this "battle of the ages."

As He was being crushed by the weight of the ominous cloud on the horizon, He poured His heart out to God, pleading to be delivered from this awful experience of death on a cross. But His greatest concern was not the brutal physical pain He was about to undergo; it was the spiritual warfare He would endure. The hosts of hell were about to have their greatest moment, and He was to be the object of their torture. He was the only man to ever live Who fully understood what they could dish out.

Yet, He had known from the beginning that *this was His purpose*. He was the only One Who could buy man back from the domination of satan–from the enslavement which had shackled the human race ever since Adam's fateful choice in the Garden. *He* was the only One Who could restore man to his original purpose of being a vessel God could live in and through in this earth. It all rested on His shoulders. He would succeed in this fight or. . . . He simply *had* to win.

But He was a man too. Could He face the physical torture without giving in? Could He carry this thing all the way through to death? Could He endure the spiritual agony of being given over to hell's hordes? Would His faith stand even to the point of death? Would that faith endure the time of death's agony? Would He trust His Father's word in the Scripture to bring Him out of the pit of death? Who had ever had to face this kind of experience? *No one!* There was no story from which He could gain encouragement. There was no fellowship of another who had walked this way before. He would be facing for all mankind the epoch battle–alone.

All of these thoughts–and many our poor minds cannot begin to conceive– pounded into His head in these moments. And while everything in His body and mind told Him to run away from tomorrow, something deep in His spirit witnessed that He must submit to this death; that He must *trust* when He couldn't *see*. And ultimately, though deserted by those closest to Him in this darkest hour of need, He chose what He had always chosen: *To do the will of God*. He chose to not just *submit to*, but to *embrace* the will of His Father.

And when He did, strength came. A special messenger from the Father appeared and touched Him, releasing strength into His weakened body and embattled mind. Now, though He had sweat blood due to the emotional pressure, His body felt much better. His mind was now at peace, as always comes with a surrender to the will of God. Joy–small, but strong–began to course through His being. He was now ready. *And the time had come.*

Chapter 4

The Epic Battle

Judas had walked with Jesus the last three years. He had even been the treasurer of the group. But there was something about him that was different from the rest. Whereas they had each been touched with the way Jesus lived and taught, Judas seemed to keep himself beyond the reach of Jesus' friendship. He never opened his heart to Jesus as the others had done. His mind had never actually changed as theirs had. Thus, his will had never been submitted to the Christ as the personal Master of his life. Jesus had been warned by the Spirit that it would be Judas who would betray Him. Now, the moment had come.

Judas stepped forward as if to plant a kiss on Jesus' cheek, the usual greeting of friends in Palestine during the first century. It was then the soldiers made their move, for this customary greeting had been the agreed-upon signal that would identify the man they were to seize.

Then it happened. As if by an unseen force, these big, strong, Roman soldiers found themselves laying on the ground. Jesus had not moved; but they had![1] All of a sudden, they began to realize they weren't dealing with an ordinary man. They got up carefully, hesitant to move again. Jesus had already asked them whom they were seeking. Now He simply agrees to go with them but requests that they would allow His companions to go free. They were certainly willing to agree to that just to avoid another mysterious "throw." All His friends quickly deserted Him, as had been prophesied hundreds of years before.

The rest of this night would see Jesus experience six illegal trials. Held at night, which was illegal for the Jewish nation to do, these first trials would be done by the local authorities. The last one would end with His sentencing by the Roman governor of the region. Only God could know the pressure Jesus would experience in these trials. For Jesus would know not only the pressure of being captive to the civil authorities of His day, but also the torture of mind-invading thoughts shot at Him from the demonic realm of wicked spirits surrounding this scene.

Indeed, hell's hordes were the real agents carrying out these trials, and they were gleeful as they sensed they now had Jesus in their grasp. They were going to take full revenge on this *God-man*.[2] He had ruled over them for years (as God had always intended man to do). Their pride had been devastated, but now they suddenly (somewhat to their surprise) again had the upper hand. Now this Jesus would pay dearly!

Meanwhile, feeling the intense pressure, Jesus is doing what He has done all through His life: He is, with each new attack, turning to the Father and, in His heart, is drinking in the Father's life. That life has strength and sanity in it, which preserves Him throughout this horrendous night. Make no mistake about it; when those accusations first hit His mind, He felt the same as you do when the enemy is attacking your mind. He felt the blows to His body just like you would feel them. The difference was, as soon as He felt them, He would–in that instant–look to the Father for another drink of His strength. (Does not *life* itself flow as a river from the throne of God?[3]) This was the way He had always lived; and He was showing us now, in the very worst mental and physical suffering, that we could still drink of the River of Life–indeed, we could have it flowing through us so that God's life could also be viewed in us.

The trials would end sometime after daybreak, but not before Jesus had felt the devastating scourge known as *the cat-o-nine-tails*.[4] As a means of punishing criminals condemned to a cross (as well as hastening their death), the Romans had devised a method of whipping, the pain of which was horrendous. But, as only God can do, He would take what man "intended for evil, and use it for our good."[5] Here's what happened:

They brought Jesus into an area of the judgment hall designed for this "scourging." They stripped Him of His clothing, so as to expose His bare skin to the lashes of the whip. They stretch His body full length, hanging him from His bound wrists, so that no part of His backside can avoid the merciless "claws" of this whip. This *cat-o-nine-tails* was designed with cutting pieces of metal or other sharp objects imbedded in the ends of its nine leather thongs. As you can imagine, a beating with this kind of instrument was so destructive, men often died in the scourging before they ever got to the cross. Jesus is hanging–almost suspended–in this exposed state, when a big Roman soldier picks up the whip and moves closer to Him. Jesus, knowing what is about to happen, looks to His Father to "drink" more of His life and faith so as to be able to endure the coming torture. All of a sudden the air is filled with the whistling sound of the whip as the soldier whirls it around his head and lands it across the back of Jesus. It connects with a thud, and those cutting "claws" in the end of the whip imbed into the back of Jesus. He flinches, but makes no outcry. Then, just as the "claws" sink into Jesus' flesh, the soldier flicks his wrist and pulls the whip in such a way that the nine thongs of the whip are drug across the back of Jesus leaving bloody trails through the flesh they had just ripped open. Then another whirl followed by more contact, more ripping, more blood.

Time after time the whip lashed Jesus. After a few minutes, all up and down His body, chunks of flesh had been ripped out, exposing the blood and sometimes the bone. After thirty-nine tormenting lashes the soldier stopped, out of breath himself due to the effort he had put into this merciless performance. Jesus, His body weakened and wracked with pain, collapses to the ground once his bound wrists are finally cut loose from their mooring.

He lays there briefly, heaving for breath, His face reflecting the horrendous pain He's now feeling. Then a course Roman soldier yells, "Get up! You've got a cross to carry." Jesus cries within to His Father for strength to get up and finish this course. By a miracle he struggles to His feet and stands woozily trying to regain His sense of balance. The soldier points commandingly to the cross prepared for Him. Jesus staggers to it–drops to one knee and *embraces* the crude, wooden structure destined to bring Him to death.

Straining to rise, He lifts the cross and begins to stagger in His weakness out into the street. Dragging His instrument of death, He sets His course for a hill outside of Jerusalem known as Golgotha–the place of the skull. The hill was so named because from a distance it bears some resemblance to the side view of a human skull. As if prophetically named, it would be the place Jesus' head would finally hang in death.

Stumbling through the streets, Jesus is watched by a tremendous crowd that has gathered. Some of them had been at His trials all through the night. Peter and others of His followers had returned to the fringes of the crowd, hoping not to be discovered, yet wanting to keep their promise to walk with Him even into death. So far their promise was unfulfilled.

Many in the crowd had seen Him do miracles even for loved ones or close friends; they too followed–at a safe distance. Some were hoping to see Him throw off this Roman yoke, symbolized to them by the cross He now bore. Some had been in the crowd who (though they had received acts of kindness from Jesus) yielded to the pressure of their religious leaders and cried out, "Crucify Him! Crucify Him!" Though some of these were regretting their treacherous action, it was now too late. Judas had been among the ones who knew deep remorse. But remorse, without repentance, equals no hope. He had already moved into the realm of fiery punishment–having killed himself by hanging.

In His weakened state, Jesus collapses under the load of the cross. Unable to carry it any farther, one from the crowd, a dark-skinned man, is compelled by the soldiers to shoulder His cross.[6] (No room for racial prejudice at this cross; we all are indebted to Simon for bearing this cross made necessary by the sin of each one of us.) Simon drags the cross up the hill to the top and drops it at the appointed place. Jesus has been following; staggering, falling, getting up again, walking a distance, then falling again. His strength is ebbing away due to the deadly beating He's just received. Finally, He too arrives at the top of the hill.

The soldiers are about their work. Three holes have been prepared into which they will sink the crosses. The other two are for two condemned criminals who are also to die on this day. Ropes are extended from the crosses to make it easier to lift them. And now the shameful process known as crucifixion begins.

The soldiers surround one of the condemned thieves. Sensing he is the first to experience the nails he starts to beg for mercy. That going unheeded and the circle of soldiers closing in on him, he begins to resist them. He fights, but to no avail. Amid his struggles and piteous cries for mercy, they nail him to the cross. He shrieks in pain, panting, gasping for breath; too wracked with pain to any longer form words. Gradually his weakening state will allow only deep groans as he can now only await his last breath.

After a similar wrestling and pleading from the second thief, he too is attached to the cross by the huge hammer and nails, and joins the other thief in creating an atmosphere too pitiful to adequately describe. The women nearby turn their heads away, unable to take in the sorrow created by such a horrible sight.

(It's amazing how the will of men, once so arrogant and violent, can be so quickly broken once they are subdued. They hurt and bleed just as other men do. What a stark reminder that for humans, *frailty is reality*. Once the mask of pride is removed, we find underneath the same weak creature common to the race. The only difference being, some of us weak creatures have agreed with God that we *are* weak [that's called **repentance**]; while others, like these two on the crosses, must be forced to display their weakness. How much better to *choose* to bow to our Creator than be *forced* to bow to Him.)[7]

Now the soldiers rest. It was hard work to kill a man on a cross. One more Man, and the hardest part of this hideous work would be done–One more.

But this One was different. Some of the soldiers had noticed the way He had taken the scourging without crying out like most men did. The soldiers who had been at the trials had noticed the way He didn't answer trumped-up charges; refusing to dignify such accusations with an answer. The times He did speak revealed His deep inner peace. He seemed to be drawing strength from a Source they couldn't identify, but yet was very evident.

However, the supreme test was about to occur.

The soldiers get up, shift their armor into place, and start to form a circle around Jesus. But then they see something that they've never seen in all their years of crucifying men. Jesus, of His own will, moves over to His cross, and stretches Himself out on it. He then extends His hands and waits for the nails. *They are shocked!* Never, among all the many experiences of crucifixion they've had, have they ever had anyone willingly accept a cross. This Man *is* different! Jesus actions seem to say, "No one takes my life from Me; I lay it down willingly." But why? Why would He *embrace a cross*?

But they didn't have time to ask questions. Besides, soldiers weren't trained to think, only to obey orders; and they had an order from the governor to execute this Man. He must have done something worthy of death. They had a job to do!

(Oh, the tragedy of acting without thinking! This is how most governmental wrongs have been accomplished: A few political schemers instigated evil while others assumed they weren't qualified to question the actions of these in such high realms of *government!*)

One of the soldiers picked up a spike. With the other hand he grabbed a mallet, then he bent over the outstretched arm of Jesus. Out of habit he secured Jesus' arm by pressing his knee against it. But with this Man there was no resistance, no pulling away as the nail was placed in His hand. The soldier, amazed that a man could face crucifixion this way, nevertheless, had a job to do.

The soldier raised the mallet, and with a mighty blow brought it down against the spike. The huge nail ripped through Jesus' hand, and the blood squirted out onto the cross piece. In a natural reflex to the pain, Jesus' arm jerked, enlarging the hole in His hand. His blood begins to run over the edge of the beam and form a puddle on the ground.

Now the soldiers hold His other arm against the opposite side of the cross. Though Jesus' body is writhing in pain, He makes no effort to remove His other arm. Quickly the spike is driven through the other hand. The muscles in Jesus' upper body are now beginning to spasm, as the soldiers move quickly to His feet.

In all this torture, amazingly, there are no shrieks of pain coming from Jesus' lips! Though He is feeling the pain the same way as the previous two men, there is the noticeable absence of the loud screams. He is suffering in silence. This too the soldiers have never before experienced. It created for them a disturbing feeling that this was all wrong. But trying to ignore this feeling, they continued their bloody work.

Another powerful blow of the mallet forces the spike through Jesus' crossed feet. His body contorts and His quivering lips reveal the pain He's absorbing—yet no sound is heard from His lips save the gasps of quickly taking in air as a reflex to the impact of the nails. His blood is now running onto the ground at a steady rate; the earth soaking up the blood of its Creator.

Yet in all this word-defying scene of horrendous torture, there is an unmistakable presence of peace surrounding this middle cross. Though unseen, it is undeniable. This Man is like no other that has ever hung on a cross. There is a Presence about Him. In spite of the cruelty, the ghastly sight of blood, and the stark disregard for human life, *dignity pervades this scene!* Something is happening here which defies description. A transaction is taking place between heaven and earth that will profoundly affect all of history.

Suddenly, as He looks to heaven, Jesus breaks his silence: "Father, forgive them. They don't know what they're doing."[8] All eyes quickly turn toward Him. What did He say, "Father, forgive them?" Forgive those who had driven nails through His body? Forgive those who had ripped His flesh with the whip? Forgive those who were wasting His very life's blood on the ground! Forgive them? Did they really hear Him right? Yet, the words were unmistakable. He was asking God to forgive the very ones who were torturing Him.

The soldiers simply could not believe their ears. They knew Jesus had been taking what they were dishing out with an attitude that they had never seen before. But when He said, "Father forgive them," He was then doing the giving out. He was stepping up to plead for mercy at the bar of judgment–for them, his tormentors. They were all affected by the statement. At least one was shaken to the core of his being. While the others tried to shake off the guilt they felt by busying themselves with gambling for Jesus' robe, this one couldn't take his eyes off Jesus. The eyes of this Man, Jesus, were captivating. Even now, as His body is racked with pain, His eyes are full of peace. While Jesus had submitted to being nailed to this cross, this soldier had the distinct feeling that He could have stopped this process, with heavenly power, anytime He chose. It was as if there were spiritual beings all around who were just longing to step in and stop this whole misuse of religious and governmental power. It seemed they were just waiting for a word–which never came.

The soldier kept looking at Jesus, taking in what they had just inflicted on a–yes–an innocent Man! He found himself admitting it deep within. This Man *was innocent!* That made them the guilty ones! Now this soldier was willing to go a step further. Could this Jesus really be the Son of the God of the Jews, as it was said that He claimed to be? What a difficult thing to imagine. Could God dwell in a human body? The Romans had tried to make their emperors out to be gods, elevating a man to the position of a god. But could God *come down to be a man?*

As all these thoughts were racing through his head, Jesus breaks in with another statement uttered in between the gasps for air and the very difficult work of exhaling. As He looks down from the cross, He sees His mother standing there beside one of His most devoted followers, who's name was John. Looking into the eyes of His mother with those amazing eyes of peace, He said, "Woman, behold your son."[9] Then looking into the face of the youthful John, He said, "Behold, your mother!" Thus, He had fulfilled His last earthly obligation. Being the oldest son in the family, it was His responsibility to see that His mother was cared for in her latter years. He was dying; thus, He gave her to a trusted friend. We're told that John fulfilled that obligation from that time on.

Watching all of this, the soldier is becoming more convinced that Jesus just might be Who He says He is. And if He is God's Son, then that fact *demands* He be listened to. If He *was* God's Son, then He would be right about everything. And if there *was only one God,* and He sent His Son to earth to be a man, that would prove He cared about us. If this was true, the Creator was evidently trying to communicate something to us humans. What could it be?

Quite some time elapsed as the soldier thought about this. Then a different voice was heard from a cross. It was one of the men condemned to die alongside Jesus that day. This one seemed to be particularly violent. In a desperate attempt to get loose from the cross, he tries to incite Jesus to do something about their plight. "If you're really the Messiah, free yourself–and us!" While Jesus remains silent, the thief on the other side calls back, between his gasps for air, "Don't you fear God, seeing you're condemned to die just like this Man? And we indeed justly." He then speaks to Jesus, "Lord, remember me when You come into Your kingdom."[10] It was then that Jesus broke His silence. With a laboring voice, He said, "Today, you shall be with me in Paradise."[11]

Thus it has been ever since Adam's wrong choice in Eden. One person is calloused toward God and His ways, allowing the circumstances of life to embitter him. Another is sensitive to God, and allows the circumstances created by his own wrongdoing to melt his heart and steer him toward God; he admits he will face God last and give an account for his earthly life, and he desires to be right with Him. One lives for earth and its fleeting rewards and pleasures. The other lives (be it ever so briefly) for eternity and becomes on earth and in eternity a useful vessel for the life of God to flow through.

For the "awakened" soldier standing beneath Jesus, this repentant thief may have become a roadmap. He could have suddenly become aware of some things he had suppressed his whole life–until now–such as knowing there had to be an intelligent Creator behind this universe. That being so, that Creator must have had a purpose in mind for all of that Creation, including man. And since man was obviously the highest being on earth, he certainly would have a noble purpose to fulfill. And he (this soldier) was one of those men. His purpose must have been pre-determined also! And if this Creator had designed him for purpose, then he surely, at some point, would give a report to his Creator as to whether he had fulfilled his purpose.

But why did he feel afraid of that? Why did the thought of facing his Creator frighten him? That's when he may have realized the repentant thief had the answer. "We, indeed, suffer justly." That was it: *We're wrong*! Doing things *the way we want* was not right after all! It was our Creator's right to tell us–*His* creation–how to live. After all, only then would we know how to fulfill His purpose for us. We were guilty of "insubordination!" *This* a soldier could understand!

By now it was noon, and a strange thing begins to happen. The sky begins to darken with an eerie blackness. For a few brief moments, the air was so still it seemed to choke you as the darkness deepened. Then the earth began to tremble. Lightning bolts were exploding against the ground. The soldiers struggle to maintain their balance, while many of the others drop to the ground, hugging it in the vain hope they can find more security in that position.

Then, unexpectedly, the voice of Jesus pierces the darkness. In a loud, wrenching voice Jesus cries out, "My God, My God, why have *You* forsaken Me!"[12]

The level of emotional pain expressed by this outcry was incomprehensible. All who heard it were arrested by its intensity. They temporarily forgot the present danger to themselves and turned toward Jesus' cross. While the light produced by the lightning bolts was short-lived, the pain in His face that they exposed was unforgettable. His brow was deeply wrinkled. The blood on his battered face was streaked with the trails of tears. One felt as if He was experiencing loneliness on a level never before known by man.

Though the initial tremors subsided after a while, the insecure feeling surrounding Jesus' cross did not. As the minutes

37

crawled by, it felt like the rejection of all the ages was pouring into Jesus. Indeed, later it would be revealed to His friends who were there that the punishment for every man's rebellion against God was being absorbed into Jesus' being in those hours. He was taking, in our place, the wrath of His Father, the righteous Judge.[13] That afternoon on the cross, He became, in every sense of the word, our *substitute*.[14]

From then on He rapidly weakened. His breathing became more labored. Exhaling became more and more difficult. In spite of the pain from the holes in His hands, He tried harder to lift Himself in order to force the air out of His lungs; then inhale with another gasp. The effort to breathe became increasingly futile.

At one point He moaned, "I thirst!"[15] One of the soldiers who had gambled for His robe, having regained some of his callous composure after the earthquake, stuck a sponge on the end of his spear, soaked it with sour wine, and held it up against the lips of Jesus. Refused the last act of kindness He ever requested from those He had created, Jesus weakly turned His face away.

Now the end was near. His breathing was so labored those watching expected death to come at any moment. But then, in an unmistakable voice of triumph, Jesus cried out, "It...is...finished!"[16] The words rang with victory, with accomplishment! It was as if His perspective on this whole ordeal was that a work was being done. The tone of His voice spoke of completing something that had been planned from eternity past. *The books were now balanced!* He had paid man's debt to God: That debt of one perfect life which man had incurred in Eden when he used, for selfish purposes, the perfect life God had loaned him. That debt was now paid. Jesus' perfect life had been offered up as a sacrifice to God to pay man's debt. The work was now accomplished![17]

A few moments later, Jesus uttered His last words from the cross. Focused on the Father, He was heard to say, "Father, into Your hands, I commit My spirit."[18] Though His body was weakened beyond exhaustion, the words rung distinctly with inexhaustible *faith!* He was entering death, but He was believing the promise recorded in Psalm 22 that God would not leave Him in death. The vision of God *would* be accomplished in Him!

With these last words, Jesus bowed His head and released Himself into the realm of death.[19]

Now it was in the Father's hands. What faith is here expressed by the Son of God! He would face all that death had to offer with only the naked faith in what God had written through prophets hundreds of years before. Here He models for us the truest example of "walking by faith, not by sight."[20] When all is said and done, the ultimate question is always: "Do I believe what is written in the Scripture?" Jesus did.

Now His followers around the cross knew they had to act quickly. The Passover was rapidly approaching, and no such spectacle as the sight of a dead body in public would be allowed. There was little time to think of the pain of grief that they were feeling. They simply had to get that body into a tomb. Joseph of Arimathea, one of His followers who was a wealthy man, had a tomb nearby. While he had intended to use it for his own burial, he now gladly offered it as a resting place for Jesus' body.

As lovingly as the urgency of the moment would allow, they lowered Jesus' body from the cross and wrapped it in a large, clean sheet of cloth. Having wrapped His head in a separate cloth, they hurriedly carried His body down the hill to Joseph's garden tomb. There they laid it on the cold stone slab carved inside the tomb, and watched as a huge stone was rolled over the entrance.[21] Roman soldiers sealed the tomb with the Governor's seal and set up their guard.

The enemies of Jesus had demanded the guard because they knew He had said He would rise from the dead after three days.[22] They didn't believe it; but they didn't want His followers to steal the body and spread a lie that He had arisen. Thus, every precaution was taken to completely snuff out the message of this Nazarene carpenter they so feared.

Those who had followed Him quickly left, uncertain as to what to do next. They finally decided to go to a certain house, seeking to comfort one another while at the same time trying to hide from the authorities. For all they knew, the religious leaders who had condemned Jesus may be coming for *them* next. Their minds were tortured with the horrendous killing of Jesus they had just witnessed. To even think of dying on a cross made their blood run cold.

As the word spread among His followers that Peter, John, and others were gathering at a certain location, more disciples came. Eventually, the entire core group was together again.

The next three days were days of painful reflection, both personally and as a group. They were desperately trying to make sense of the recent events which had ended in Jesus' death. They were now afraid they may have been wrong about Him being the Promised One. All the while, they were fearful of what the next opening of the door might bring. They were afraid to go out–but afraid to stay here. They were simply–*afraid!*

Each day passed in tearful grief and painful questionings. As the weekly Sabbath day came to a close, their questions were no more answered than they had been three days ago when they watched Him die. Tomorrow was just as uncertain. Oh, *why* had He died!

Chapter 5

Alive!

One of their group, Mary Magdalene, was just as uncertain as the rest. However, the love in her grateful heart would not be denied: Not by questionings *or* by fears. Jesus had set her free from a wretched life of bondage to sexual sin and the torture of evil spirits.[1] *He had changed her!* She had never been the same since that day she met Him, and her gratitude of duty now compelled her to go to the tomb and do the anointing with spices to His body, which time had not allowed the day He died.

Though it was still mostly dark, she gathered her spices and started to make her way to the tomb. Some of the other women fell into step with her, but Mary was oblivious to their presence. She only vaguely heard the question about how would they ever be able to roll away the stone from the tomb entrance. That stone over the entrance weighed several tons. It was *designed* to keep out intruders. And then there was the Roman guard. Would they still be there?

Her grateful heart refused to be slowed by these questionings, and it kept her moving along the way toward the tomb. How painful it was to think that just four days before, Jesus had been dragging that crude cross over these same streets. The images that were burned in her mind brought painful tears to her eyes. Oh, why did some people hate Him! It was beyond the comprehension of her honest heart to think there could be anyone who wouldn't love Him. He had been so good! Why did He have enemies?

But just now they were starting on the path to the tomb. Mary's heart began to race. Her knees felt weak, but she refused to slow her pace. Then she saw it!

The tomb had been opened! The Roman soldiers lay on the ground completely motionless. Her feet immediately stopped;

and it felt like her heart would too. Then she saw him–or whatever *he* was! He was sitting on top of the huge stone that was the door of the tomb. They instantly knew that the removal of the stone had been *his* work. *He* had been the one who immobilized the soldiers. Unable to go further, the women stood frozen in their tracks.

Then the being spoke, "Don't be afraid. I know you're looking for Jesus, Who was crucified. He's not here. He is risen! He is risen *just like He said He would!* Come, step inside the tomb, see for yourself."[2] Now some of the fright seemed to subside, and Mary found herself moving toward the entrance to the grave while the other women followed. She peered inside. He was right! Jesus' body was gone!

The women filed into the tomb one by one. They stood there absolutely amazed, questions flying through their heads. All of a sudden the tomb was filled with brilliant radiance. Another being–no, two of them–were sitting on the stone bed: One where Jesus' head had been, the other at the feet. These creatures were so majestic the women fell on their faces before them. Bowed low, the women heard them say, "Why do you seek the living One among the dead? He is not here; He is risen. Remember how He spoke to you while in Galilee, telling you He would be killed by sinners, but on the third day would rise again."[3]

The light they were bowing in seemed to sink into their souls. They remembered! Now it began to make sense. He had told them this. He had said it was all part of the Father's plan. He must die–but He would come back to life again–after three days!

One of the angels interrupted their thoughts by issuing a command: "Go, tell His disciples–*and Peter!*"[4]

While the words were not harsh, they were authoritative. Mary obeyed. She got up, and shielding her eyes from the brightness, she stumbled out of the tomb and then began to run back to the house. The other women followed closely on her heels.

Racing through her mind were many questions, but they couldn't eclipse the one burning thought that was gripping her: Peter and the others had to know the grave was opened! She wondered how the men would react if they told them the angels–yes, those beings must have been angels–had said Jesus was alive? These men were heartbroken. Some were angry. Would they listen to *women* telling them someone was *risen from the dead*?

Bursting though the doorway, she and the other women who had seen the opened tomb began to pour forth words like a gushing spring. Trying to talk over their companions with increased volume, it took several long moments for their message to be understood. The big fisherman couldn't believe what he was hearing. The tomb was opened? Who? How? Why? The questions immobilized him, but not young John!

The impetuous youth bolted for the door! He would see for himself! Peter, letting his curiosity overcome his questions, followed suit, and caught John by the time they entered the street. They ran together toward the tomb, shouting the questions in their minds as they ran along. After a distance, the difference in their ages began to show as Peter began to fall behind, panting for breath.

The women overtook him and joined him in his half walk, half run to the garden where the tomb was located.

John's youthful stamina propelled him onward, and he arrived at the tomb several moments before the others did. It was as the women had said: The stone *was* rolled back and the entrance to the tomb was open! He slowly moved closer, stopping at the threshold of the entrance. He could now see clearly the grave clothes lying limp on the stone bed where they had laid Jesus' body three days ago. But where was it now?

As he was thinking on that question, Peter and the women arrived. The women noted that the angels were no longer visible. Never known for his timidity, Peter didn't stop at the opened doorway of the grave; he barged right in.[5] He stood there looking at the empty linen cloth. There was no mistake here. The empty head wrap was right at his hand, close enough to touch. It was like the head had somehow been removed without disturbing the winding strips of cloth. Jesus' grave clothes were here, *but His body was gone!*

Dazzled, Peter stumbled out of the grave, almost knocking John down, who by this time was standing inside the tomb also. John was staring at the stone bed with the linen wrapping when he began to feel his heart warmed. Suddenly He remembered Jesus had said He would rise again *from the dead* after three days. The three days were now past and here were empty grave clothes! Could it be? Could Jesus now be alive again! He turned and followed Peter down the path toward the city; and as incredible as it all seemed, John now found it easier to believe Jesus was alive than that He was still dead. He didn't voice it. He didn't have to. He believed it!

As the women saw Peter and John leaving the garden area, they decided to follow, still reluctant to tell what the angels had said. *Surely, if He was alive…*

Mary did not want to leave. She stood there a few steps from the entrance to the grave, trying to sort out all that had happened. The angels had said He was alive. Jesus Himself had told them He *would* come back to life. But could that really be?

She moved closer to the entrance. Questions were flying through her mind. Could He really be alive again?

She didn't know how long she stood there lost in thought. She finally decided to look again. As she took steps toward the tomb she was suddenly overwhelmed with grief again. Tears started pouring from her eyes, obscuring her steps. She stumbled closer, wanting to see again the empty grave clothes on the stone bed where Jesus' body had lay.

As she put her head on the doorway and wept, she was instantly blinded with light! There they were again! The two shining creatures they had seen earlier or–two just like them.

They looked at her with compassion. "Woman, why are you weeping?" they asked. "Because they've taken away my Lord and I don't know where they've put Him," she wailed.

She turned her head away, having no stamina which could stand up to the questions of celestial beings. What had happened?

Where was His body? Her mind was racing, exceeded only by the racing of her heart.

Blinded by tears, she turned from the doorway and nearly bumped into a figure standing there. In between her sobs, she heard the person say, "Woman, why are you weeping?"

More questions! Everyone kept asking her questions. Oh, who would dare intrude at such a moment as this? She was tired. She was confused. Couldn't somebody just tell her where Jesus' body was!

Anyway, who, at this hour, would be in this Garden? Then a thought seemed to force its way to the surface of her thinking. Could this perhaps be the caretaker? It must be. Surely, no one else would be here this early. Maybe he had moved the body–or knew who did.

In childlike faith, so typical of a distraught woman, she fell at his feet, grasping his ankles and pleading, "Sir, if you have done something with the body of Jesus, please tell me. I'll come and take it away," her tears revealing her deep sincerity. Her sobbing face was lying on his feet, the hot tears running over them.

"Mary!"

The voice! It was–Oh could it be–*that voice!* It was the voice that had first spoken peace to her tormented soul. It was *the voice* that had driven out the evil spirits that had bound her. *It was Jesus' voice!*

She turned her tear-stained face upward to see those kind eyes looking down at her with tenderness and compassion. *It was Him! He was alive!*

"Master! Mary exclaimed, hugging His ankles with all the strength in her. She had found Him again–He *was* alive!–and she wasn't about to let go of Him. "Oh, Master, Master!" she cried. The joy flooding her emotions knew no bounds! Her tears of pain were now turned to tears of joy: Joy greater than she had ever known!

Jesus gently said to her, "Stop clinging to Me. I'm on the way to the Father. Don't detain Me now. But go tell my brothers that I'm ascending to My Father, and their Father, too. I'm going to My God, and their God."

And after a moment, He was gone. She had just had His ankles in her hands–and now He was gone! But what should have been a loss didn't feel that way now. He _was_ alive! Mary had the distinct witness in her heart that He wasn't gone forever–that He wasn't far away. She rose from the ground and began to run to tell the others. They must know. *He was alive!* Just like He said, He had gone into death and come out of it at will. *He had overcome death!* He was not *only* spirit. She had held the ankles of His new body in her own hands. *He was flesh and bone again!*[6]

Chapter 6

Accepted! Delivered! Victors!

What Mary didn't see in that Garden was the host of others who were there. The many believers from the past who were standing around Jesus, waiting for the most triumphant entry ever staged. They were the "spirits of just men made perfect."[1] Abel, Noah, Moses, David, Daniel and many, many others. They did not yet have their new bodies, like the one Jesus had. But they knew His was the certain promise that theirs would one day come.[2]

He was leading them from Paradise (the place where they had been at rest ever since their death) into heaven. The Father in heaven had ever wanted them with Him, but something had to happen first. Since all the spirit realm operates on legal principles,[3] there was a legality that must be taken care of before they could enter the Presence of the Almighty God. That's what this train following Jesus in His ascent to the Father was all about.

As they reached the gate of heaven, they found it opening to them. Light more brilliant than the mind can conceive shines from the other end of this main street of heaven. The angels bow and worship, announcing the return of the Son of God. Jesus strides toward the end of that street. Onward He goes, amidst the praises of all the hosts of heaven. He walks right up to the throne of the Almighty, Creator God, His Father. And then, the most sublime act in all of history is done by Jesus: He simply stretches His hands toward the Father, palms up, presenting the blood of His fresh wounds.

The Father takes those hands in His own. With tenderness He holds them, gazing at them with all-knowing eyes. All heaven is absolutely still. There is no movement, no sound anywhere. All eyes are on the hands of Jesus held by the Father's own hands. Eternity seems to hang in the balance. The destiny of every human being is about to be revealed.

Then, in a resounding voice that shakes the very foundations of heaven, earth, and hell, the Father states: "It's enough! It's enough, Son! One sacrifice for sin for all time. The debt is paid in full!"[4]

The Father now looks toward the faithful believers waiting at the gate. "Let them come," He shouts! "Let them come and join us in the coronation of My Son." His eyes return to Jesus. Respect as only God can give was seen in the Father's eyes as He looked on Jesus in that moment. Exaltation resounded in the Father's voice as He said to Jesus, "Come, sit here at My right hand while I make Your enemies Your footstool."[5]

Jesus is seated on the Father's right side while all the waiting believers rush to the throne.

A thunderous shout of praise echoes over the hills of heaven! It reverberates throughout heaven and hell! Earth was brightened in that moment with the hope that man could be restored to all that God originally intended him to be.

All is now right. Mankind is redeemed; bought with Jesus' own blood. The debt of one perfect life which man owed to God is now paid. Jesus' perfect life was offered up to God as a sacrifice that the debt might be removed.[6] There is now no barrier between man and God. Jesus' offering removed it![7]

Jesus' death also worked deliverance in another way. Ever since Adam chose to go his own way (what God called 'sin'), mankind had been plagued with disorder in his bodily desires. God-given desires, designed by the Creator for His own glory and our own good, had actually become the agents of bondage. The desire for food, sex, rest, exercise and other desires of the body and mind had been mixed with the *sin principle* (In the Scripture this is called the "old man." [Rom. 6:6]). The "I–want-what- I-want-when-I-want-it" attitude had ruled these natural body desires much of the time. The stirring up of these desires by satan's hosts had brought all the pain and destruction recorded throughout the history of man. That which was designed to bring life had actually been a channel of death and disorder.

48

But Jesus' death had righted this disorder! While He was hanging on the cross, God had worked a miracle concerning this "old man." As only God could do, He fused this "old man" into Jesus. Jesus had carried it on the cross—until He died. But when His body died, our "old man" died with it.[8] It was now dead! It could now no longer demand of man his allegiance. *Something dead rules no one!*

This act would become the channel of deliverance for future followers of Jesus. Now those who, in the moment of a particular temptation, would *believe* their "old man" died, would find the energy of sin draining away.[9] Without the "old man" as a gateway into the internal workings of man's soul, satan's work *inside* man was completely defeated. Internally, man could be free![10]

This truth would become one of the distinguishing marks of Christianity. Whereas the only hope of any semblance of deliverance in other religions depended totally on the *self-discipline* of the individual, in Christianity there was a *supernatural* deliverance worked through the individual's belief in Jesus' putting to death the "old man" at the Cross. In any given temptation to misuse bodily desires, all the believer must do was to *believe,* at that moment, that this inordinate desire died in the cross. From the moment true belief was exercised, he would find the energy of the temptation draining away. (Hallelujah, what a Deliverer is this Jesus!)

But yet another victory was won by Jesus. This one was worked by His resurrection.

When Adam sinned in the Garden of Eden, he received the sentence of death. This was legally right since "the wages of sin is death."[11] Death had reigned over men.[12] Within the limits of God's Sovereignty, satan held the power of death.[13] Death became satan's weapon to stop the desire of God for man to be an "earth-suit" of His life.[14] Every individual who could be led into eternal death (hell), was an individual that would miss the purpose of God. It was one more person in whom the glory ("heavy presence") of God could not reside. This is why satan "walks about as a roaring lion, seeking whom he may devour."[15] This is the reason his mission is to "steal, kill, and destroy."[16]

But when Jesus descended into death,[17] He took on the greatest weapon Satan had. He "tasted death for every man,"[18] experiencing the full penalty for sin. Then, of His own will, He chose to come out of death, thus displaying His power to "lay down His life, *and to take it up again*."[19] He proved that the life of God is greater than the death satan used. It's why John, who believed at the empty tomb, would later write, "Greater is He who is *in* you than he who is in the world."[20]!

In breaking the greatest weapon satan had, He broke the devil's power forever.[21] The "accuser of the brothers"[22] can now *only accuse: He has no real power to affect believers*. Only if we walk in ignorance ("My people perish for lack of knowledge." [Hosea 4:6]), or choose not to believe what God has said in a particular situation, can he enslave us.

When Jesus ascended out of death, satan's defeat was eternally worked. It's why Paul would later challenge death with the question: "O death, where is your sting? O grave, where is your victory?"[23]

Jesus eternally freed us from the fear of death, which is what satan had used to enslave men.[24] Jesus has "freed us, indeed!"

The stage is now set.

Jesus has paid man's debt to God. God can now legally accept man in His Presence. His fellowship with God is now legally restored.

Jesus has delivered man: Both from himself, and from enslavement to his "old man." It is now possible for man to overcome the "I-want-what-I-want-when-I-want-it" attitude in his natural bodily desires. Internal victory can now be reality!

Likewise, Jesus has completely and eternally broken satan's dominion over man by defeating his greatest weapon, death. Satan can no longer force man to live in the fear of dying.

Through Christ's work, death, for the believer, has become nothing less than a gateway into the visible Presence of God. What we've known here on earth only by faith, we can, through death, know in visual reality: "Behold, every eye shall *see* Him..."[25]

Through the matchless work of Christ, we are now legally accepted by the Father! We are now delivered from the "old man!" We are now victors over our arch enemy, satan! Now only one thing remains.

You'll remember that God made man "in His image, after His likeness, to have dominion..." *in this world*. God's desire from the beginning was that man should "look like Him, live like Him, and rule like Him" *in this earth*. However, this could actually be done only by God Himself since, in reality, only God can be like God. Remember, too, that this is why God made man a three-part being. The Trinity wanted to inhabit this creature called man. Literally, man was designed to be an "earth suit" in which God could live and move about, thus expressing His own life *in this world*.

Now that man is restored to his original position with God, how does he get the life of God into him so he can become what he's created to be? And if the life of God *could* indwell an individual, why couldn't it indwell a unit of individuals–like a family, or a church? And if God could indwell a family and a church body, why couldn't He indwell a community? And if He could indwell a community, why couldn't His life be the driving force of their institutions like education and government? And if His life could be the driving force of a local community, why couldn't His life be the driving force of a nation? Could the dream be possible–could a nation exist for the purposes of God? Could America... That's "the rest of the story!"

Chapter 7

Proof and Presentation

For the next forty days Jesus goes back and forth between heaven and earth.[1] Often, He is seated at the Father's right hand. But occasionally He comes to earth and becomes visible to His followers.

That first day He appeared to Mary, then to two disciples (one of whom was named Cleopas) walking down a road.[2] He then became visible to Peter and the other disciples later on that day He was resurrected.

A little over a week went by and He again suddenly became visible to a gathering of the disciples. Thomas, who had been absent at the other appearances, was now present. Initially skeptical of his friends' reports that they had seen Jesus and that He was alive from the dead, he now exclaims, "My Lord and my God!"[3] One *personal* experience of the *living* Christ is always more valuable than all the combined experiences of others with Him.

Later, Jesus appeared to over five hundred of His followers at one time.[4] Five hundred people cannot possibly spread the same story, and have it remain the same, *unless it's the truth!* It was simply now undeniable that He was raised from the dead. It's interesting that, from the records of the first century, no scholarly rebuttal of His resurrection has ever been found among secular writings. One would think that if any flaws in the reports by His followers could have been uncovered, it certainly would have been.[5]

The last appearance recorded during these forty days was a conversation He had with them about when the kingdom would be restored to Israel. He plainly stated to them that this understanding was reserved in the Father's mind.[6] Their concern was not to be the restoration of the nation of Israel, but rather the restoration of man. They were to focus on telling what He had accomplished by His death and resurrection.

They were to keep the main thing the main thing!

During His final appearance, the last thing they remembered Him saying was, 'All authority has been given to Me in heaven and in earth. Go on this authority. Go into all the world and tell everyone this Good News: *They can be what they were created to be!*[7] I've fixed it! Go tell this Good News: You *can* believe! And if they *will* believe in Me, they can be delivered out of any bondage, and become all I created them to be!'

Then, as He was speaking with them, He just started rising off the ground. Slowly, steadily, He ascended upward into the sky. As He became smaller and smaller to their sight, they strained to catch a last glimpse of Him. And then He was gone—*at least from sight.*

Startled by a voice, they turned to see two angels standing there. They said, "You Galileans, why are you standing here staring up into the sky? This very *same* Jesus, Who has just been taken up from you into heaven, will come back to earth in this very same manner in which He just left."[8]

The words were so comforting! He would be back. Yes, they *would* see Him again. But right now, they had a job to do. He had told them to go back to Jerusalem and wait for the Father's promise of the Holy Spirit. So they started down the mountain toward the city. They weren't quite sure what "the Promise of the Holy Spirit" meant, but they figured when He showed up, He would be too obvious to miss. They were right!

Chapter 8

God's "Earthsuits" – Man Is Restored!

Jesus' followers had been together a lot during those ten days. They had done a lot of reflection on the things they had heard Him say and do. They had shared their viewpoints with each other as to what all this meant. They also opened their hearts to each other in a way they had never done before. They found themselves sharing their greatest desires for the future, both personally and what they hoped for this kingdom Jesus had spoken of so much. Likewise, they shared their deepest fears with one another; those things you just don't tell someone until you *really trust them.*

Just as Jesus' appearances to Peter and to Thomas had caused the fear and unbelief to drop off them, now reflecting on His different appearances somehow made it easier to bare one's thoughts–the *hopes* and the *fears*. This opening of the heart began to work a oneness, a unity among them that made them feel as if they were a real part of the others. They were becoming more than just a group of believers meeting in the same place. They were becoming an actual *body* of believers, joined together by the same thinking, moving in the same direction.

They had decided to come together on the Day of Pentecost. This was one of the traditional Jewish Feasts that was celebrated at the beginning of the new wheat harvest. Among other things, it was for the purpose of reminding the Jewish nation of how God gave the law at Mount Sinai in a tremendous display of His power. Moses had climbed the mountain and met with God for forty days. In an awesome display of power, God engraved, on the rock of that mountain, words that summed up His mind. He then cut the rock into two tablets and split them from the rock bed, giving them to Moses. God's awesome power had been displayed in revealing to man written words that revealed His own thoughts about Himself and His creation. On these tablets were written God's standard for man's relationship to Him, as well as his relationship to his fellow man. Now, His awesome power was about to be seen again.

Through the prophet Ezekiel, God had promised that one day He would take away the hard heart of man and give him a teachable heart. One day He would dwell inside man so that He *Himself* could be seen through an individual's life. Since God gave the Law at Mt. Sinai, man had struggled to keep that standard. Over and over he had failed. So God had promised him that, "I will put my Spirit within you and *cause* you to walk in My statutes; you *will* keep my judgments and do them."[1] What man, in his best will power, could not do, God was going to do *through* him.

It happened on the first day of the Feast. They were gathered together as they had often done since Jesus' return to heaven. All of a sudden the room was filled with the sound of a powerful wind. Fire appeared and began to come on each of them! It was impossible to remain still! They were stirred to cry aloud; and when they did, languages that they had never spoken before flowed out of their mouths. They could tell something was happening inside of them. They were ecstatic with joy! And there was power–power to be what they had been created to be! Boldness immediately replaced fear. This must be the coming of the Holy Spirit which Jesus promised them! His power was being felt throughout the room and it could not be contained.[2] Some of them began to go down the stairs and out into the street. There they met with their second surprise.

They had not been the only ones to hear the sound of the massive wind. People in the street were evidently hearing it too. Scores of them had gathered to what seemed to be the center of the sound. Others were running from all over the immediate area to the house where the miracle had occurred. As the sound of the wind subsided, they heard Jesus' followers speaking in languages which the speakers had never learned. Some were skeptical and began to accuse them of being drunk. It was then that another shock occurred.

Peter, the disciple who just fifty-some days before had denied his Lord three times when Jesus had been on trial, stands up and begins to address the crowd. All fear gone, Peter refutes their idea that this group is drunk. He points out it's only nine o'clock in the morning. It's too early to be drunk!

He then begins to explain to them that this is what God had promised through the prophets. This was the promised Holy Spirit Who could empower them to be all God had created them to be! He then points out their sin in crucifying Jesus. Without mincing words, he puts the blame for Jesus' death squarely on their shoulders; but then tells them that it is possible for the Holy Spirit to live inside them also. This promise is also *for them and their children*! There is no compromise in Peter's newfound boldness. His was no message of "I'm okay, you're okay." Yet his message was one of complete hope. If they would admit they had thought wrongly about Jesus being God's Son, about themselves, and about their fellowman, they could have the Holy Spirit come to live inside them. If they would admit they had run their lives without acknowledging that it was actually the property of the God Who created them, they could be delivered from what they had become.[3] God's new work could begin inside them, changing their heart and mind. They, by the indwelling life of God, could be made into what God had created them to be!

It was a message of hope and many responded by receiving Jesus as God's Son and the promised Messiah. Then it happened to them too. They were born anew in their spirit as Jesus, in the person of the Holy Spirit, came to live inside them. They were changed from that moment and began to experience the peace and purpose they had so longed for all their lives. Three thousand were baptized that same day as not only Peter, but the whole group of original believers began to move through the massive crowd, boldly telling them that Jesus was the promised Deliverer–that they too could have Jesus step into their bodies and, by His indwelling Holy Spirit, produce His life through them. Aided by the Holy Spirit, they spoke the particular native language of each person listening, which greatly helped to convince the crowd that this was indeed a work of God.[4]

The change in thousands of lives that day was too much to keep a secret. Not that they were trying to! They went throughout the surrounding area telling people that not only was Jesus alive, but that He had come to live inside them; and that he wanted to live inside *all* people. That He wanted to "put on that individual as an earth suit" (so to speak) and live His life through them, became their theme. To many the hope that they could be what God had created them to be was "water to a parched heart." They drank it in. Then they were changed and went out to tell others of this great hope.

Over the next three hundred years, they became carriers of Jesus to others all over the world.[5] So much so that it's estimated that before the fifth century, half the known world had heard of Jesus. Multiplied thousands of lives were changed. They were becoming what God had created them to be–a channel of His life. The impact of this release of Christ's life through believers affected every part of the culture.

Building strong families and educating their children from the principles in the Bible produced generation after generation of people who were examples of morality and wisdom in the midst of an ever-decaying Roman society. The followers of Jesus were like lights in a dark world, holding high Christ Himself as the answer to all the searchings of mankind, and the cure for all the ills in society.

The fraudulent Roman courts began to be replaced by a Christian court system, the decisions of which people voluntarily accepted because it was so much more just than the Roman courts.[6] Justice reigned among believers, which brought order to their subculture, in stark contrast to the growing anarchy in Roman society.

Some Christians began to advance even in the government. Their attitude that they were the people's servants, instead of their masters, cast a new standard for government service. Their honesty and fair mindedness quickly gained the respect of the people. Government began to be seen as the ministry of God to preserve His order in society, instead of being viewed as the tool of wicked men to control the masses.

Not that these believers were always perfect–not at all. There were some miserable failures in the city of Corinth. These were not men perfect in the flesh. Not all who joined with them had actually experienced the new birth and the indwelling of the Holy Spirit. The actions of these hypocrites greatly hindered some who were considering the message of hope that the true believers were telling with their lives and lips. Jesus had told the original group it would be like this, so it came as no surprise.[7] Sometimes the judgment of God was quickly and openly exercised on these pretenders, as was the sudden death of one couple in Jerusalem named Ananias and Sapphira. At Peter's word they dropped dead on the spot because they had knowingly lied to the Holy Spirit.[8]

When occasionally a true believer did stray from his Master, the discipline exercised by the withdrawal of the group of believers caused him to quickly return to the fold. The separation from the group rapidly produced a repentant heart. The world was too cold for a real believer to want to stay there very long. The warmth of real acceptance in the body of Christ (i.e., believers) was a powerful drawing force to effect his quick return.[9]

This powerful flow of the life of God through believers was the fulfillment of God's dream for man to be a vessel of His life in this world. That first day the Holy Spirit came to live in them, He had revealed to the teachers among them that the group had literally been made the body of Christ.[10] He had immersed them into the life of Christ. They were now His dwelling place, His body in this earth. God was now living through man, doing *what* He does in the *way* He does it.

While God, Christ, and the Holy Spirit were thrilled with the overall scope of things, there was *one* who was not thrilled. The diabolical enemy of man was in serious trouble. His old line to the minds of men–that they couldn't possibly be what God had created them to be–was working less and less. The more men saw the love and faith of the Christian community, the more they were believing the message that God had a plan for their lives too. They, in turn, would change their mind about God and Christ, receiving Him as their Master. They, too, would experience this new birth of Christ in their spirits and become a vessel His life could flow through, and the process was then repeated all over again.

Satan, the enemy of God and man, was loosing his strangle hold on the human race.

From his perspective, the situation simply could not be worse. He could envision, if this continued, his whole kingdom in this world falling apart. The world system, built on pride and selfishness which he had so labored to build was in danger of collapsing. Something must be done! This must be stopped! The devil simply could not allow man to discover that, by the power of the indwelling Christ, *he could become what God created him to become*! He must keep this from spreading. Why, whole regions, or even *nations,* might become carriers of this message, unless he did something now!

And he did have a plan…

Chapter 9

Counterfeit Commitment: The Truth Is Suppressed

Satan had always wanted control. His attempt to take over God's throne in heaven was the very reason he was cast down from his original position as the worship leader of heaven.[1] Once he was defeated in his attempt to gain control of heaven, the next best thing he could do was to try to gain control of earth. Given the rule of earth by Adam, its God-ordained master, satan had rapidly entrenched his deceptive ideas in earthly governments. *Since civil government is the greatest natural power among men, government was Satan's greatest opportunity to control the masses;* and keep them in the bondage of deception. But he knew if this message that Christ could dwell in man and live His life through a human, was allowed to spread, the truth would overthrow his rule in earthly governments. If mankind ever discovered that the original Legislator, Judge, and Executive (Is. 33:22) was living inside of them, they would then discover that they, the people, were the rightful authority *for*, and the best source *of,* government on this earth. Satan could never allow this to happen!

He first tried to stop this movement with persecution. He used the Roman government to mercilessly mistreat Christians, eventually making them the hunted prey of hungry lions. Thousands would fill the Coliseum to watch innocent believers fight the vicious lions loosed upon them. It became great sport to Roman citizens to watch Christians thus torn limb from limb in these horrendous events. Satan's strategy was to stamp out this Christian movement by saying to all who viewed, "This is not worth it. Don't become a Christian!"

But just the opposite happened. The more Christians laid down their lives, forgiving those who were working their death, the more others admired them. In turn, many of them gave their lives to Christ. They acknowledged that they too wanted a cause worth dying for. And this was more than *a* cause: This relationship with God was the very reason they had been created. The selflessness of the martyrs testified to them that Jesus was *alive in them*–that He could walk inside one even in "the valley of the shadow of death."[2] Satan's persecution of the church simply caused it to grow. He found himself being used by God to achieve the very purposes of the Almighty! *How frustrating to fight against the Sovereign God!*

When persecution didn't work, he resorted to his old tactics. Satan has always been the master of deceit. From Eden he's tried to convince man that God is not trustworthy. He has constantly tried to make us believe that God does not have our best interest at heart.

He again mixed error with the truth, convincing church leaders that they too were being "short-changed." The church was missing the help of a lot of "good" people by insisting all had to repent. He suggested to them God's way was too *exclusive*. He accused them of *narrow-mindedness*: It wasn't right to insist that people *repent* of their attitude toward God in order to be a part of the church. That was too *harsh*. They should try to *include* everybody. After all, didn't God create us all? Are we not *all brothers*? It was *bigotry* to insist that only those who were born again were part of the Body of Christ in the earth.

Besides, the church was missing out on a lot of talent that could be very entertaining in their meetings, if only they weren't so *narrow*! And then, of course, there was the matter of *income*! Didn't the church need money for all the good things it was trying to accomplish? There were lots of *good* people out there who would be glad to contribute–if only they could have a little "say" in what direction the church should go. Other organizations seem to thrive without demanding such a strict standard from their members. Surely the church could too.

And weren't the times *different* now than when Jesus had been on earth in the first century? This was the late 300's; surely some changes were in order. Why should *only* the Bible be looked to as the rule of practice in the lives of church members? Hadn't the Greeks produced *superior* thinkers without the Bible? It surely wasn't the *only* book of wisdom!

Thus, with his deceit, he convinced church leaders they should take the world into the church. The Roman emperor had all his citizens baptized into the church. The church's numbers soared! Now the church was *popular–and wealthy!* It "was rich and increased with goods and had need of nothing"[3]–except *power!*

The power was now gone. Soon the power to overcome sin was a lost experience. The power to command satan and his host was gone (he doesn't *take orders* from within his own ranks–he *gives orders!*). The ability to move God by prayer was gone from all but a handful: That few maintained their purity before God, *and through them He continued to walk in this world.* But most were swept away by the compromise, and within a generation or two, the knowledge of God and why He had made man was lost. And mankind began to sink into the mire of unbelief.

Separated from the Source of Knowledge and Wisdom, mankind quickly lost ground in education. From the year 380 to 1380 fewer and fewer people learned to read. Ignorance and superstition reigned. Mankind went backwards in every area of civilization. Science advanced very little. Medicine retreated into superstitious treatments that resulted in the average life ending by 35 years of age. Economic life was stifled causing widespread poverty. There were a few super wealthy land barons while the average person barely kept soul and body together. Most governments were controlled by the few, while the many were greatly oppressed. Class systems, which always develop when the selfish nature of man is allowed free reign, became so entrenched it was next to impossible for anyone not born to "nobility" to ever better his oppressed lot in life.

Mankind could hardly have been in a worse state. *But–*God had a plan. He saw in His mind a different kind of nation just down the road a ways. However, what lay between now and then would be very costly. A tremendous price would be paid to give birth to that nation.

Chapter 10

God's Instruments of Liberty

God's plan had not changed, even though man had left the good beginnings brought about by Jesus' death, resurrection, ascension, and outpouring of His Spirit into believers. Still yet, God had not given up on His dream of man being a vessel He could live His life through. And He was about to do something major to get man back on track with His purpose.

He had been preparing a man in England to be His vessel in this next move. It was the mid- 1300's. John Wycliffe was a professor at Oxford University. He was a Godly man who was grieved by the wrong he saw all around him. He saw the hypocrisy so rampant in the Church–in leaders as well as followers. He saw government administered by men eaten up with selfish ambition. He saw people suffering from sickness. Wycliffe had watched the Bubonic Plague kill over a third of the population of Europe. Men were oppressed by sickness and poverty simply because they didn't know the truth taught in the Bible about health and how to prosper in this earth.

God birthed in John Wycliffe's heart a dream of changing all that. He believed that the Bible had the truth, not only about how to get to heaven, but also how to live life *now in this present world*. He knew if he could just get the Bible into the hands of men, God would use His truth to bring them back to Him. They would start turning to God. The new birth would then bring the indwelling Christ into their lives and they would, by His power, start changing according to His Word.

But how could he do this? Even if he could manage to get the Bible into the hands of the common man, how could he make him understand it? Very few people, even among the nobility, could read. If they were to understand it, either they must be taught to read, or someone must read and explain it to them. Wycliffe decided to use both these methods to accomplish his God-given vision.

He left his position as professor at Oxford and became the Pastor of a small church. His aim was to free up his time so as to be able to use much of it for translating the Scriptures into the English language. Though it meant considerable sacrifice of financial and social standing, he gladly embraced his new setting because he believed it was the Lord Jesus' method of bringing men back to Himself.

His commitment was contagious. Others began to join him in getting out portions of the Scripture to people all over England. These followers came to be called Lollards. The term means "idle babblers." It evidently was pinned on them due to their method of teaching people to read the Scriptures they were giving to them. It seems certain they used phonetic sounds to teach people the skill of reading.[1]

The method worked. Wycliffe completed his translation of the Scriptures in 1382. And before many years had passed, half of the English population had turned to Christ and aligned themselves with the "Lollard movement." Their fervent preaching and distribution of the Scriptures brought new understanding to the English population of who God was and what His plan for them was. Revival fires began to burn all over England because of the Lollards' faithful sharing of the Scriptures with their nation.

In his process of translating the Scriptures into his native tongue, John Wycliffe discovered a truth that would change the course of history. It would shape all of western civilization and become the cornerstone of government in the United States. He was so impacted by it that he insisted on it being copied into the introduction of each Bible which his followers distributed. He wrote, "The Bible is for the government of the people, by the people, for the people."[2] He had discovered it was the Bible that taught that the common man should rule himself.

Man must first, by the power of Christ, rule his own appetites and make them the servant of God. Then he must control his *civil* government as well. By the same indwelling Christ, wisdom could flow through a disciplined individual which could enable him to "choose wise and...discerning men...of truth who hate dishonest gain,"[3] to represent him in government. Wycliffe had discovered that God never intended for the many to be ruled by the few. Rather, God desired that self-rule (internal government) should extend from the inner man (his spirit) all the way into *civil* (external) government. Thus, the rule of God in a man's spirit could, potentially, extend to the farthest reaches of the culture, including civil government.

Wycliffe's belief that the "Scripture must become the common property of all"[4] became the driving force which gave birth to the Protestant Reformation. His translation, and the work of his followers to distribute it and its message, lit fires in the hearts of Englishmen that would never die. Eventually, that fire would spread to a Catholic monk by the name of Martin Luther, and would begin to blaze brightly in Germany and the rest of Europe. This is why John Wycliffe has been called "The Morning Star of the Reformation."[5]

Wycliffe's translation of the Scripture hailed a new day in which men began to think with God again–before they thought with other men. Thinking independently of the "fear of man" began to be widespread with the completion of Wycliffe's Bible. Thinking with God according to the Bible (instead of thinking with the world system) began to be that which would later become the primary source of ideas about education, government, and economy in the Western world. Men ablaze with zeal for the truth of God to be implemented in every area of the culture began to teach Biblical principles about the *institutions* of the culture as well as the personal life. In their communities they demonstrated the practicality of these principles by creating cultural institutions based in Biblical truth.

The life of man began to improve steadily as Biblical truth spread in Reformation fires.

The foundational laws of science were identified by Issac Newton in the 1400's, who credited God with those discoveries.[6] Medical and technological discoveries were the fruit of that. New discoveries meant the development of new products and better transportation methods. New products meant better markets and thus lifestyles improved.

All of this betterment in man's life came because of the rediscovery of truth: The truth about why God made man and what His purpose for man was. When man knows his purpose and is rightly related to God, peace is always the result. When a man is at peace, his mind readily thinks with God. God's creativity flows through him and thus, he comes up with better and better products and methods.

However, not all were happy about the truth rising in the culture. Many rulers in the church and in the civil realm desperately clung to their positions. They didn't want the common man ruling and leading in society. Many Reformers paid the supreme sacrifice of a martyr's death in order for the truth to come to their nation. Our debt to them is inestimable.

However, other Reformers were protected by God and allowed a long life with which to shape their nations. The improvement in the liberty and lifestyle of those nations was a hint of what was to come. And on the horizon there was the breaking gleam of a different kind of nation.

One of those who would live the full length of his life, though often sought by those who would quickly have killed him, was Martin Luther. Luther was a German law student who turned to the priesthood as a result of revival fires now burning in Europe. In his early years as a priest, he struggled with the accepted Roman Catholic idea that God was an angry God Who needed to be appeased by the religious works of man. This often translated into money paid to the church for "indulgences," which were supposed to release men from punishment during this earthly life, or from "purgatory" in eternity. In practical terms it meant that men could do what their passions dictated if they would pay the Catholic church money.

But not all men agreed with this outrageous scheme. Martin Luther was one such man. His sensitive conscience drove him to search deeper into the Scripture to find if man's relationship to God was based on his own works, or on the work of God alone. And since God promises, "If you seek Me, I will be found of you,"[7] Luther had a revelation from God. In the course of his reading, he came across the statement in Romans 1:17, "The just shall live by faith." It exploded in his thinking! The "just" live, not by their works to try to appease God, but by "faith" that Jesus has already "fixed it" when He took our sin into Himself at the cross and suffered in our place. He paid our debt once for all![8] Our punishment was taken by Him! He already gained God's approval *on our behalf!* Our faith in Him releases us from all fear of hell. Therefore we *live by "faith," not by fear!*

Luther's discovery brought him into the new birth, and he was forever changed.

He would never again try to appease God's anger against his sin by doing religious things. He would trust the finished work of Jesus Christ at the cross to make him acceptable to God. And he would believe that because of Christ's rising from the dead, the power of Christ was resident in him to make possible the living of the Christian life.

Because Luther saw how people were kept enslaved to religion through the demands of deceived church leaders, he began to cry out against the man-imposed rituals of the Catholic church.

On October 31, 1517, he tacked a document to the door of the Wittenburg church in Germany containing ninety-five statements identifying many false ideas taught by the Catholic leaders. This event would change the course of history. Through Luther's courageous act, the "liberty of conscience" would be restored to men.

As the German people considered his revealing statements, they began to break with false ideas in the Church, just as John Wycliffe had done 150 years before. Their courage would inspire others to again think with God instead of blindly accepting what deceived church leaders were teaching them. Revival fires spread across Europe causing men to throw off the yoke of religious tyranny and to start again to teach the truth to the next generation.

And while they were not perfect in their methods, they had made that very necessary break with the false religious system that had held men in bondage for centuries. That gave others the courage to go back to the Bible for the truth, instead of just accepting without question a church leader's ideas. And before many years would pass, there would be the forming of a group which would walk out individually, and culturally, the truth of the Gospel.

That group, who will be identified as the *Pilgrims,* would enact the very principle Luther stated concerning dealing with government authority when that authority was resistant to the truth:

> *"Do not dispute with the prince for place. Let the community choose their own pastor, and support him out of their own estates. If the prince will not suffer it, let the pastor flee into another land, and let those go with him who will, as Christ teaches."* [9]

One such man has been rightly called the "Father of America." He would be the next torch in the spread of the light of liberty. That light would ultimately see, in the birthing of America, the greatest expression of civil liberty thus far.

Chapter 11

Seeds of A Biblical Republic: Internal to External

John Calvin was a Frenchman who had a heart for truth. He, like Wycliffe, believed the Bible was the source of all truth on this earth. Though he lived a century and a half after Wycliffe, his method of getting out the truth was similar. He fervently shared the light he had with a crowd, or with one individual. But because it was God's time, the numbers who flocked to him grew all through the years. Persecuted in France by the established church, he fled to Geneva, Switzerland, where he established a teaching ministry. Like the Bereans in the first century, the crowds who flocked to him gladly heard the Scripture taught. And his teaching would revolutionize western thinking.[1]

While Calvin is recognized as one of the greatest theologians in all of history, the impact he made on his culture around him is often overlooked. He did more than establish schools. He shaped the government of Geneva into a solid republic. Law was based on Biblical principles, and a greater degree of justice than ever before was achieved. In His *Ecclesiastical Ordinances* he taught how to improve education, sanitation, and jails.[2] It may be that the cleanliness of the Swiss, which has become a hallmark of that people, owes its beginnings to the Genevan Reformer.

His principle of "Renovation" taught that the spirit of man must be made new. He echoed the words of Jesus, "Except a man be born again, he cannot see (perceive) the kingdom of God."[3] Calvin believed that man had been permeated with sin and thus, must be changed to become what God intended man to be. To know God, he taught that you must be more than just a member of the church. One must personally accept Jesus' death and resurrection as the only means of being forgiven and changed into the likeness of God. One must acknowledge God's right to own his life, since He made him and provided his redemption.[4] This would cause one to be born again, and thus have his spirit come alive to God. God literally indwelt that person who had been born again. Thus, God could begin to produce His life through them.[5]

Further, Calvin taught that the study of, and obedience to, the Word of God was the only means by which a person's mind could be renewed to "think with God." We must agree with God that He has the right to teach us to think with Him, otherwise our thoughts would be controlled by the world system. It was our only hope of becoming a vessel God could live His life through in this world. And this "renewing of the mind" was more than just thinking with God about one's own needs. It must also include every area of the culture.

While Calvin believed in heaven and hell as places of man's eternal destiny (depending on what man did with Jesus), he also insisted that our *present life in this world* was a gift from God to be used only for His glory. He would never have tolerated the current idea pervading so many conservative churches–the idea that this world is a place to be only tolerated while we think of the heaven to come. He believed firmly that we must take dominion in this world as Genesis 1:26 reveals. *This* is his much-overlooked usefulness in God's overall purpose.

His view of our purpose in this world could be summed up by a simple, little phrase attributed to him. That is, "internal to external." What did he mean by "internal to external?"

Calvin believed that the internal change, which occurs when someone acknowledges God's right to rule their life, and invites Jesus to step inside and begin that rule, must be allowed to grow outwardly. This internal change, which we call the "new birth," affected the way men thought. This happened because Christ, Who was now within them, began to release His thoughts through them.[6]

Because their thoughts began to change, their actions also began to change. Thus, the external life, the part which we see, began to change into what God had always intended. Worship of

God began to replace self-centeredness; acts of kindness replaced selfishness; love replaced bitterness, and so forth.

However, Calvin was different from most of his predecessors of the middle ages. While a number of theologians had taught that the external actions must change, they had placed the focus of this exclusively on the individual life. Calvin now began to teach that we must let this internal change grow outward toward more than just the individual and family life. He began to emphasize that God deserved to rule the institutions of the culture just as He deserved to rule the individual life. In effect, his teaching was that the educational, economic, and governmental institutions must also come under the discipline of God. God's law must be the foundation of all our civil law.[7] Otherwise, no matter how much men changed personally, satan could still rule a nation through a handful of individuals who were in key positions of the educational system, or the government.

This belief that God had a "form," as well as a "spirit," of government would change the course of the western world. Men came from all over Europe to learn Calvin's views of God, the individual, and the culture. Through his leadership, the little Republic of Geneva became a great example of what could happen when individuals who were born again participated in every area of the culture. That example would have great affect on America.

In the mid 1500's our earliest Puritan forefathers went from England to Geneva to learn from John Calvin. They came back to England and Scotland with the firm conviction that the internal change they had personally experienced must be allowed to grow to the furthest reaches of the culture. The truth of the Bible, which had so reshaped their lives, must be allowed to reshape the institutions of their nation.

Education must be reshaped to teach the Biblical *why* as well as the *method* of teaching children. The economy must be reshaped to *support* that education system. And the governmental system must be reshaped to *protect* that education and economic system. Government and economy must reflect the same structure *and* spirit that was shaping the education system. The cultural institutions must promote and protect the idea that man was *made* in the image of God, *redeemed* by the Son of God, and here to *accomplish the purpose* of God.

This was the simple, yet profound teaching of the Genevan Reformer. It would chart a new course for the Western world.[8] This simple concept of *internal to external* would become the foundation of the thinking of a segment of the Puritan movement (which segment we shall see more of later) in England. (It would also greatly influence the Scottish Presbyterians, under the leadership of John Knox. This would greatly influence the birthing of the American Republic in the late 1700's.) From Calvin they had received the firm conviction that this internal change, which Christ had worked in them through the new birth, **must** be allowed to grow into the institutions of education, economy, and government. That segment of Puritans would eventually be called *Pilgrims*.

Because that small group of people would find that they could not purify the decadent Church of England, they would *separate* themselves from it, establishing new churches. These new churches were structured according to the original church in the Book of Acts. Their *covenants* insisted on a way of life which the Bible revealed as being normal for Christians—a life where Jesus was *Master* of every part of the life. And since He was Lord of all, they believed Him to be the rightful and able *Ruler of government*—that, "the government should be upon his shoulders."[9] Thus, He, through those He indwelt, could best choose the rulers for both the church and the government. It was the same principle that John Wycliffe had discovered over 150 years before: "The Bible is for the government of the people, by the people, for the people."

However, these *Separatists,* as they were first called, would find that the monarchs of England didn't think the government needed reshaping: It didn't need the people's voice. Neither were they hesitant to use their tyrannical powers to try to squelch such thinking. Allied with willing Anglican Church leaders, these tyrants would harass the *Separatists* until their only choice would be to leave England.

Thus, the birthing of America was looming on the horizon. However, more preparation was needed for this group to become the parents of *"the land of the free."*

Chapter 12

Shaping the Minds Which Would Shape a Nation

With the fires of revival flamed by the death of martyrs burned at the stake, many Englishmen were questioning their current religious system. Had these martyrs been just heretics who deserved a death by burning? Or were *they* the people of *substance*, and the religious leaders who engineered their death the *hypocrites* who were outside the truth? Many became convinced this set of religious leaders were no better than those of Jesus' day who had engineered His death.

As these *seekers of truth* searched the Bible, they "had their sins discovered unto them"[1] (as one of their number would later record), and began to turn to Jesus as the One who could deliver them from themselves, and shape them into all they were intended to be. One after another began to experience the "new birth," and their spirit came alive to God. They had discovered that God could live *inside them*![2] They were astounded to find that God was real *in this world*! They found the Bible coming alive to them as they discovered they had been forgiven and restored to become the individuals God had created them to be.

This was no average church members' experience. This was not adding God to the life as another responsibility–another obligation to fulfill. This was experiencing moment to moment the resurrected Christ *alive in* them, living His life *through* them. They had found the *meaning of life*!

This new *personal* relationship with Christ became the focus of their conversations with others. And sharing together with others who likewise had experienced this "new birth" became the greatest joy in this world. This redefined the meaning of *family*. They came to see that those who knew Christ personally were their real family.

Thus, the *Separatists* (they would later be known as *Pilgrims*) entered a *covenant* in 1606.[3] Because, as a result of their personal study of the Bible, they had come to think alike, they entered an agreement "to walk together in all His ways, made known, or to be made known to them, whatsoever it should cost them, the Lord assisting them."[4] *Covenant* means the "meeting of minds." Their consistent study of the Word of God had more and more brought their individual minds into agreement with the mind of God. The more they *individually* agreed with God, the more they *corporately* agreed with one another. This made possible their moving together as a unit: *And* it would shortly become the basis of both *church* and *civil* government.[5]

Their discovery of Biblical truth would cause them to conclude that they must *separate* from the Anglican church. Thus, the movement that would result in the birthing of America, would begin in a small farming community called Scrooby in north central England. The world would never be the same again.

These *Separatists,* as they called themselves, began to meet *in their homes* for worship. They wanted to be free to express their love to God in songs not known to traditional English methods of worship. They wanted to pray freely (which sometimes meant loudly), as they were prompted by the indwelling Spirit of God. They desired to be taught the Scriptures verse by verse, having their children sit at their feet and likewise learn from their Pastors, who were very knowledgeable men in the Scriptures. From the Scriptures these leaders would teach them how to structure a family, a church, and a community.

Their leading Pastor was John Robinson, "a man not easily to be paralleled," who was "of a most learned, polished, and modest spirit."[6] Another who had considerable influence among them was William Brewster, who would later be their Pastor in America. He would be described as "their special stay and help."[7]

The noted historian, George Bancroft, would record, "A clear and well-written apology of their discipline was published by

Robinson, who…as the champion of orthodoxy…disputed in the university with such power that, as his friends assert, 'the truth had a famous victory.'" [8]

These Puritans believed they could only know this kind of worship and teaching by "separating" from the established church. Though this meant leaving friends and many memories, the prize was worth the price.

However, this separation was not welcomed by the Anglican church leaders. Their idea of being a church member was a holdover from the Catholic idea of the middle ages, which taught that God spoke to church leaders only, and that they were the only ones who could tell you His ways and His will for your life. The Separatists believed God could indwell *each* believer, and thus could speak to any individual who knew Him, anytime He wanted to.

Those presently in power thought this idea was dangerous to a monarchy. It meant men would begin to think of themselves as equals with their rulers. Not only did this threaten the comfort and position of *church rulers*, this meant *civil rulers* would be expected to listen to their ideas–the ideas of *common* men! Government "of the people, by the people, and for the people," was simply unthinkable. This must never be!

Thus, persecution of the Separatists began. At first it was only threats. When that didn't bring them back into the fold, economic pressure was used against them. When it became obvious that the Separatists were so closely knit as a "family," they would take care of each other (not to mention the many outsiders who sympathized with them and helped them), soldiers began to intrude into their home meetings and drag their leaders off to the magistrates to be fined. When that method failed, jail sentences were added to the fines. Separatist leaders often spent thirty days or longer in those jails; their only crime being they wanted to worship in a different way. Open ridicule was then added in an effort to not only affect the adults, but their children as well. Even when they began to go deep into Sherwood Forest to worship, in the hope they could freely sing and preach, the Sheriff's *hounds* "sniffed" them out. However, none of these methods persuaded the Separatists to abandon their new church meetings.

As the persecution grew over several years, it became obvious something must be done. The Separatist congregation together made the heart-wrenching decision they must leave their homeland. The emotional turmoil this created is hard for us to grasp. This had been home for generations. Furthermore, they were tied to the soil. Almost all of them were farmers. The land that fed, housed, and clothed their families had done the same for their parents–and their parents before them. Generations had gotten their living from these lands. Their blood and sweat and labor hallowed these grounds. The thought of selling it was like selling the very life of their ancestors!

And yet, Jesus *had created them and given His very life's blood for them.* They owed their very breath, not to mention their newfound peace, to Him. Viewed in that light, no sacrifice was too great to make possible His liberty being passed on to their children.

After considerable prayer, they decided to go to Holland, since others in the Separatist movement had already found much more liberty there than in England. Thus, in the fall of 1607 they made their first attempt.

But leaving England in those days was not as easy as travel is today. Aside from having to sell their farms and hire a ship to take them to Holland, it was against the king's law to do so. The king wouldn't allow them the freedom to worship God in their own way, but neither would he let them leave the country. Thus, since that law disagreed with the Bible, they decided to leave without his permission. They believed the law to be in disagreement with the will of God; therefore, they could disobey it with a clear conscience, though they did so with no flippant attitude. They broke civil law only in the gravest of circumstances. This *was* one of those circumstances. As Peter and John had set forth the principle before the civil authorities of their day–"We must obey God rather than men"[9]–so these Separatists were determined to obey the higher law of obedience to God, even if that meant being disobedient to the laws of man.

Having agreed to pay an English sea captain to take them to Holland, they boarded his ship on an appointed day in an isolated spot on the eastern coast of England. But no sooner did he have them on board (and had collected his fee) than he called for hidden magistrates to come out of the hold and arrest them. They did, confiscating all their goods, even searching the women "beyond modesty," as William Bradford would later write.

Thus, in one's day time they lost the work of generations of their ancestors. It was the sell of their farms that had furnished the money with which to make the trip; that money had now been taken into the king's treasuries. We can only imagine the heartbreak they felt at this loss, not to mention their present distress of having no place to go and no way to make a living. But they had found Jesus Christ to be their Redeemer and Shepherd, and they believed He would take care of them. Their hurt was real, but their faith was greater than their hurt. And as Bradford would later record in their history: "But these things did not dismay them (though they did sometimes trouble them) for their desires were set on the ways of God and to enjoy His ordinances; but they rested in His providence, and knew whom they had believed."[10] They found His Providence (defined by Noah Webster as *The care and superintendence which God exercises over His creatures.*[11]) to be ever watchful over them. Somehow, they made it through till the next spring, when they hired a Dutch sea captain to take them to Holland.

Though the 1608 voyage to Holland was not without its challenges (They were hounded by both weather and magistrates.), at length they all arrived there safely. To finally be reunited with family and friends in a country where they could worship in freedom inspired "no small rejoicing,"[12] as Bradford would describe it.

However, they now faced an enemy uncommon to them. Their men had intended to work in the Dutch factories in order to make a living (Holland's economy being based on industry, not agriculture, like they had been used to). But to their surprise, they found that Dutch labor unions had managed to get a law passed in Holland, which kept immigrant men from working in their factories. And it mattered not if you were a legal, or an illegal immigrant, the labor union had "walled" you out of the economy.

This was a frightful situation. Most all of their money had been spent (or confiscated by the King of England) in just getting here. They had no reserve to fall back on. They knew they had to find work immediately or else watch their families starve. But they prayed and trusted God. He had led them here, and surely He would provide some means for them to earn a living.

But the "test" would run long. Though the men worked every waking moment at odd jobs, they simply could not earn enough to make a living for their families. The "wolf" was already at the door; and the day was fast approaching when he would be *inside* the house!

There was one other possibility, but it was so dreadful they refused to consider it in the beginning. The Dutch law, while not allowing immigrant *men* to work in their factories, would allow immigrant *children* to work in their factories (though, no doubt, at greatly reduced wages). However, the Separatist parents dreaded the very thought of this. It would mean their children would be exposed to the "ways of the world" in a very liberal Dutch society. To throw children into such adult influence could only hurt them. Even if they survived the immoral influences in the factory, the work would be hard and of such long hours that the children would age before their time; and what was worse, they would not receive the Biblical academic education their parents had come here for the purpose of giving them. This latter reason being the very most important reason they had come to Holland. If they couldn't teach their children concerning Christ and His plan for their lives, their main ministry as parents was lost. They were *in Holland* mainly for their children to be able to know God and His plan for them. How could they release them to work in such an atmosphere?

Over time, however, it became evident they no longer had a choice. They must let some of their children go to the factories, or they would go under financially. They finally agreed to this, only because there simply was no other way. The men were working frantically to establish their own woodworking businesses so they could market their products on the "black" market. Their children's work in the factories was only for the purpose of buying time for the new businesses to get established. Though eventually it worked, some of these parents' worst nightmares were realized.

Some of their children were so influenced by the adults in the factories that they got sidetracked into worldly amusements and vocations. Some went to sea and were never heard from again. A few left the faith of their parents altogether. This was the worst of pains for these parents. All other troubles they had known were as nothing compared to the thoughts of their children being lost to the cause of Christ, *now* as well as in eternity. It's really difficult for us to comprehend such wounding of the soul, since most of us today are so far removed from their depth of commitment and their understanding of the ways of God.

And yet, they persevered, because of their own relationship with Jesus Christ, as well as for the sake of the children of other parents in their group. While in England they had dreamed of being free to worship God and teach His ways to their children. They now had religious freedom. But they were learning the hard lesson that without economic and educational freedom, you could not pass that religious freedom on to your children. Though the loss of a few of their own children was the terrible price of gaining this understanding, this knowledge would free millions in the future to have opportunity to become all that God had created them to be.

Because of this, as well as other pressing reasons, the group began to consider if they shouldn't move somewhere else: Somewhere where *they* could control the government, the economy, and the education system. They had come to realize personal knowledge of Christ was not enough to guarantee the liberty of the next generation. If they were to pass on their knowledge of Christ and His plan for their children, the principles Jesus had taught must also be allowed to shape the *institutions* of their culture.

Not that they wanted to force others to submit to their way if they weren't willing to vote to establish that way. These were people who had already suffered more than most for what they called "the liberty of conscience." They didn't want to force anyone's will. They just understood that believers must stay in the majority in the political realm, so their vote would control the institutions of the culture. Otherwise, laws would be enacted on the basis of human reasoning. The result would be that the sin principle, at work in those who didn't walk with Christ, would eventually destroy the liberty of all but a handful of "elitist rulers." *They knew civil liberty was the fruit of religious liberty.* Civil liberty could only be maintained by the freedom to proclaim the Gospel of Christ in all its implications for the institutions of the culture, as well as for the individual and his family. This was their stated purpose for going somewhere else.[13]

Thus, after much prayer and debate in their church gatherings, they decided on going to America. It seemed like a desperate move to many onlookers. America was a wild country full of untamed animals and many savage Indian tribes. Even if they could live through the trans-Atlantic voyage (which most didn't), how could they possibly survive in the American wilderness?

Only a people with a deep faith in Jesus Christ could answer such a question with quiet confidence. These Separatists, who would later be called Pilgrims, *were just such a people.*

Their thinking about life and eternity was not the thinking of the average person. For years it had been being shaped by the Spirit of God through their Pastor, John Robinson. That it was far beyond the thinking of their day (and we could truthfully say, our day as well) was revealed by the wise *Farewell Letter* their Pastor wrote for them.

Here we encounter the spiritual depth of Pastor Robinson. His knowledge of God, as well as man, is recorded in this letter, written to those of his flock who were making the voyage to America. Though he would not get to take the voyage with them (the larger part of the flock being left in Holland, causing him to feel he must remain behind) he assures the voyagers he will be with them in spirit, and sends with them his earnest instructions. Given with the humility and care of the wise, spiritual father he was, he would give his final word to them on July 22, 1620 from the deck of the *Speedwell*, the little ship taking them to England to meet the *Mayflower*, the old freighter which would be their means of crossing the Atlantic.

He first addresses their need of walking in honesty with God. He writes:

"And first, as we are daily to renew our repentance with our God, especially for our sins known, and generally for our unknown trespasses...Whereas...sin being taken away by earnest repentance and the pardon thereof from the Lord, sealed up unto a man's conscience by His Spirit, great shall be his security and peace in all dangers, sweet his comforts in all distresses, with happy deliverance from all evil, whether in life or in death."[14]

Next he addresses the importance of their walking carefully with one another so they neither *give offense* nor *take offense* as a result of their daily transactions with one another. He states,

"And...your intended course of civil community will minister continual occasion of offense, and will be as fuel for that fire, except you diligently quench it with brotherly forbearance."[15]

And then he reveals his insight into one of the most subtle devices of satan in his work against man. He warns of the danger of listening to deceptive accusations against the very person and nature of God Himself. He writes,

"And if taking of offense...easily at men's doings [is to be] so carefully...avoided, how much more... that we

*take not offense at God Himself, which yet we certainly
do so [often] as we do murmur at His providence in our
crosses, or bear impatiently such afflictions [with which]
He [be pleased] to visit us. Store up, therefore, patience
against that evil day, without which we take offense at the
Lord Himself in His holy and just works."[16]*

He then reveals his understanding that they are created as a
vessel through which God can express Himself in this new land;
he warns them not to let their life together be built on any ideas
that would hinder the flow of God's life through them. He cau-
tions:

*"And as men are careful not to have a new house shaken
with any violence before it be well settled and the parts
firmly knit, so be you, I beseech you, brethren, much
more careful that the house of God, which you are and
are to be, be not shaken with unnecessary novelties...at
the first settling thereof."*

Finally, their beloved Pastor reminds them of the governmental principles that are a part of every mature believer's life.
First in their personal and family life, but then in their church and
community life, Biblical government is to be shown. He reveals
their understanding of the principle of a *republic* at work in them
personally and as a group. He writes:

*"Lastly, whereas you are become a body politic, using
amongst yourselves civil government, and are not furnished with any persons of special eminency above the
rest, to be chosen by you into office of government; let
your wisdom and godliness appear, not only in choosing
such persons as do entirely love and will promote the
common good, but also in yielding unto them all due
honor and obedience in their lawful administrations, not
beholding in them the ordinariness of their persons, but
God's ordinance for your good; not being like the foolish
multitude who more honor the gay coat than either the*

virtuous mind of the man, or glorious ordinance of the Lord.[17]

"These few things therefore, and the same in few words I do earnestly commend unto your care and conscience, joining therewith my daily incessant prayers unto the Lord, that He who hath made the heavens and the earth, the sea and all rivers of water, and whose providence is over all His works, especially over all His dear children for good, would so guide and guard you in your ways, as inwardly by His Spirit, so outwardly by the hand of His power, as that both you and we also…[may praise] His name all the days of your and our lives. Fare you well in Him in whom you trust, and in whom I rest."

An unfeigned [wellwisher] of your happy success in this hopeful voyage, John Robinson[18]

In the days ahead they would read Pastor Robinson's *Farewell Letter* over and over again to remember why they were doing what they were doing. It would help them remember *"in the dark*, what they had learned *in the light."* For *"the dark"* was close upon them.

Chapter 13

The Evidence of Providence

It was September, 1620. An old freighter was anchored in Plymouth Bay on the southwest coast of England. It was to be the "sea home" of the Separatists who were crossing the Atlantic for America. (They had been forced to abandon their smaller ship, the *Speedwell,* because of leaking) She wasn't luxurious, but she was sturdy. That was important because the *Mayflower,* as she was called, would be carrying one of the most precious loads a ship ever carried. Not that these 102 *Pilgrims*, as they would later refer to themselves, had much in the way of earthly goods. They were still, for the most part, common tradesmen who were not at all wealthy by the world's standard. They earned their bread by their skill in their hands, just like thousands of other Europeans did. What made them so valuable to the future of the world was the vision they held in their hearts. Because, as we have seen, they had come to know Jesus Christ in a personal way, they carried His vision for a new nation. One in which His people would control, with their votes and their Biblical wisdom, the educational, the economic, and the governmental systems of this new nation they were planting. They dreamed of planting a community on American soil that would allow each individual the opportunity to become what God had created him to be. They would be equals, esteeming only those who would walk in the law of God as being worthy of the honor of leadership. They, themselves, would decide that as they worked, and worshipped, *and wept* together. And because of the pressure they would shortly endure, they would have ample opportunity to do all three. They were about to come to know each other well enough to know who was real in their profession–and who wasn't.

The pressure of adversity was needed, because about one fourth of their number had been forced upon them at the last moment by the businessmen who financed their trip. These "strangers," as the Pilgrims thought of them, would be tested to the "max" very shortly. This would have to be a quick work, because in little more than two months, they would be living in the American wilderness–the first European *families* to establish a community here. Whether they and their little ones survived would be dependent on how well they obeyed the laws of God in the Bible. The Pilgrims already knew His way worked. They had been walking in it for 15 years. But these *strangers...*

The first part of their voyage was blessed with fair weather and wind. They were halfway across the Atlantic in 30 days. Aside from being seasick and the horrendous cursing the sailors hurled at them, their voyage was better than they expected.

One sailor in particular spit out venomous profanity, cursing their God and threatening them by saying, "You're all gonna die. Landlubbers always die on these voyages. And I can't wait to slide your dead body over the side of this ship and feed you to the fish." It made their blood run cold, but they treated him with Christian respect and never returned his insults. But they knew he was right about the death rate. Most people, except sailors, who boarded a ship to cross the ocean in the early sixteen hundreds never saw the land where they were going. *They did die.* Mothers hugged their children tightly, trying to assure their little ones that they would be okay.

They did *believe* they would be okay. They were undertaking this voyage, as they would later write in the *Mayflower Compact*, *"for the glory of God, and the advancement of the Christian faith."*[1] Surely, their Jesus would see them through!

Then an event occurred that sobered them all–and stopped all the abusive speech the sailors had been throwing at them and their children. One morning, that most blasphemous sailor who had so threatened them with "feeding them to the fish," took sick with a fever. No one else caught the fever–just him: And, *he died before nightfall! His body* became the very first one to be slid over the side of the ship and buried at sea. The captain and crew recognized this as the hand of God judging that sailor. They said so! *And* they stopped their cursing of the Pilgrims.

A second happening served to show them just *how much* God was with them. As they entered their second month at sea, the North Atlantic began to live up to her reputation. Horrendous storms began to engulf the *Mayflower*. Mountainous waves washed over her deck time and again. The captain ordered all who were not seamen below deck.

That, in itself, was enough to drive the average person crazy: 102 people crowded into a space less than half the size of a basketball court; weeks on end without a hot meal; never even seeing the light of day; and no place to throw up (from the constant seasickness), except down into the hull of the ship. The same was true of "toilet functions." One tiny "candle lantern" cast dim light in an ever-rolling, stinking inferno. The stench alone was enough to make you lose your sanity. Evil spirits shouted, "Death!" to them at every creaking of the ship.

Those who didn't know God very well quickly discovered their true selves; and they (as well as others) did not like what they saw. Those who did know Him well, though hurting too, gently, persistently helped the others to face their sin. And as they did, God helped them *repent,* and they too came into the "joy of the Lord"–and unity with the others. They discovered that circumstances do not dictate attitude–unless we let them!

But then it happened. Suddenly, a tremendous *boom* was heard! Startled, they frantically looked around for the cause of such a resounding noise. Even in the dim light, it only took one look.

The splinters sticking out from a center beam revealed a huge crack in one of the most important timbers in the ship. Though not seamen, they knew if this stabilizing beam broke in two, they would go to the bottom of the ocean in a matter of minutes. Thus, they were already praying for God's deliverance when the hatch burst open. The captain and crew had likewise heard the mighty sound and feared what it might mean. Upon their first glimpse of the beam, their worst fears were confirmed. Frantically, some sailors started trying to move it back into place while others hurried to get some timbers to aid them. But neither their strong arms, nor the leverage of the timbers, could budge the broken beam. Death was staring them in the face.

But at this darkest moment, someone remembered there was a giant "screw" onboard.[2] Quickly, they made a diligent search for it among the baggage. It was shortly found and hauled up to the spot under the broken beam. With this great "screw" the sailors were able, amid great crackling of wood, to push the beam up into its proper place. And the *Mayflower* made the rest of the voyage with that main beam, though cracked, holding the main mast steady.

The *most* amazing thing about this incident was that this "screw" was supposed to have been left in England! When the businessmen had added some twenty-five people to the Pilgrim numbers, they had been forced to make room for them by leaving some of their belongings that were intended for the trip (including this screw) on the dock. However, *someone* (human or divine, and the Pilgrims never knew which!), had loaded this giant screw, thinking it *was* supposed to be a part of the cargo! Thus, the screw was there when they needed it.[3]

Finally, in November, they heard what they had yearned to hear for so long: "Land Ho!"

They had been blown way off course to the north, but considering all their circumstances, they decided this must be where the Lord intended them to settle. They dropped anchor just inside Cape Cod.

But though they longed to be on land again, before they would get off the ship, they did one of the most important things of their entire lives. Their men met together and wrote what would be called the Mayflower Compact. It would be their governing document. In it, they first stated their reason for coming to America: "In the Name of God, amen. We whose names are under-written...Having undertaken, for the glory of God and advancement of the Christian faith...do by these presents solemnly and mutually in the Presence of God and of one another, covenant and combine ourselves together into a civil body politic..."[4]

It was the first time in recorded history that common men chose their own form of government. It was a Biblical Republic, the same form of government they had used in their church for 15 years. Law would be the highest authority. That law must be in agreement with Biblical law and must be the willing choice of the people, expressed by their vote. That law would apply to all, leader or follower. In principle, it would become the form of our state and national governments 150 years later. Men, under the leadership of the indwelling Christ, would make their own laws and, by the power of His indwelling life, obey those laws. As renowned historian, George Bancroft, would so correctly analyze it: *"In the cabin of the Mayflower humanity recovered its rights, and instituted government on the basis of "equal laws" enacted by all the people for "the general good."*[5] Thus, America was birthed as a *Biblical Republic.*

When they finally got off the *Mayflower*, though their urge was to run and jump on the sandy shore, the first thing they did was to kneel and pray. They had begun this voyage many weeks before by kneeling on the dock in Holland where they had left the rest of their church family (who hoped to join them soon). They ended it with a thanksgiving prayer to the God who had brought them across this "vast and furious ocean" now at their back. They were committed to their God. They had trusted Him to get them here safely. He had. Only one had died, while the average death rate was 90% with others who had tried such a voyage. And as a seeming promise from Him, a baby had been born on the voyage. Thus, by miracles, 102 landed-—the very same number that had left England over two months before.

However, their situation did look bleak. There were no lodgings, no friends to welcome them with hot meals. As far as they could see, only the bleak, November shoreline of this new land greeted them. William Bradford, their governor for 35 years, who would later write their history, added a fitting description of their present situation. He wrote that he was "...amazed at this poor people's present condition…Having thus passed the vast ocean…they now had no friends to welcome them, nor inns…to refresh their weather-beaten bodies…Summer being done…the whole country…presented a wild and savage view…What now could sustain them but the Spirit of God and His grace?"[6]

They were about to learn in a deeper way than they had ever known that, "His grace is sufficient."[7] Grace *alone* would sustain them.

Chapter 14

The Pilgrim Commitment
Plants a Christian Republic

Tired or not, the Pilgrims had to find a place to live. And that was no easy task. Their small boat, called a *shallop*, had been taken apart in order to fit into the limited space they had on the *Mayflower*. She had to be reassembled before they would have a vessel with which to explore this place. Between the exasperating work of putting her four parts back together, and unfriendly encounters with the Indians, the next month was not a pleasant experience. And worst of all, death entered their ranks in December and took five of their number. Deeply saddened, but with no time to grieve, they daily explored Cape Cod's shores trying to find a suitable place to build their village. They prayed earnestly God would guide them.

Near the end of December, He literally "blew" them into the narrow opening which is the entrance to what is now known as Plymouth Bay. In a blinding snowstorm, their little boat was blown off course and wound up inside the Bay on what came to be called Clark's Island. The next day when the sky cleared, they could see across the Bay the land that is now Plymouth, Massachuetts. When they rowed across the bay, they would find the land that would become their home. They were so impressed with the lay of the land, along with its soil and its four fresh water springs, they knew they had found a home.

The great mystery was that this land had been previously cultivated. By whom and when they didn't have time to try to find out. As for now, it seemed to belong to no one; so some of them immediately set to work building their houses, while the rest went back to tell those still aboard the *Mayflower* what they had found.

But with the full blast of cold winter air upon them, the work went slowly. Finally they had the walls of their church building up, which gave some protection from the cold wind, even though the roof wasn't finished. They began to carry their sick and dying into it, building a large fire in the center in the hopes they could manage to stay warm enough to survive. While those well enough worked diligently to finish the roof, others fell to what they called the General Sickness. At one point there were only five men well enough to tend the sick and dying, as well as work on the other houses which would be needed. Those five also showed up for guard duty just in case there were any Indians watching from a distance.

Many of the Pilgrims succumbed to death. Before the winter was over, 50 of the 102 who came, would be laid in their graves. Fearing an attack, they buried their dead at night in unmarked graves to keep the Indians from knowing that their numbers were dwindling.

Why were they willing to go through such suffering? What was important enough to them to lay down their lives like this? It was the same purpose for which they had endured religious persecution in England. It was the same reason for which they braved the economic persecution in Holland. They wanted *their children to have the liberty to hear and live the Gospel of the Kingdom of Christ!* And they wanted *them* to be able to *teach their children* that same Kingdom Gospel! They were living for the *next generation, not themselves!*

Later, when Governor Bradford would write their history, entitled *Of Plymouth Plantation,* he listed their reasons for coming here. Among those reasons, and no doubt the main one, was that they had, *"A great hope and inward zeal...for propagating the Gospel of the Kingdom of Christ in those remote parts of the world, even though they should be but stepping stones unto others in...so great a work."*[1] They came here for the purpose of teaching the Gospel of Jesus Christ, first to their own children, and then to their neighbors, the Indians. They did this to both groups with remarkable success.

You see, they understood something the last few generations in America have not been taught: Namely, that *all liberty flows out of religious liberty.* Being able to freely study the Bible and "think with God" (which is what the word "reason" means[2]), allows Him to teach us His principles of liberty. *And God is about liberty!*[3] And though that understanding begins with the *individual*, it must not be allowed to stop there: The Bible is also the source of the teaching about *civil* liberty for the family, community, state, and nation! The communicating of the Gospel to the next generation was what the Pilgrims were about. We must be about it also–*if we want our children to live in liberty!* What a tragedy if we waste the most precious gift in this world on fleeting pleasures! How will we be able to stand before God, as we surely will,[4] and justify it?

By March, 1621, the Pilgrims needed a miracle. They simply were starving to death. The food supplies they had brought with them were exhausted. Their hunting and fishing efforts were mostly failures. Outside of God's intervention, the dream of planting a community of liberty in the new world was about to die. So now, they did what they had done for many years: They prayed to God Almighty in the Name of Jesus Christ, pleading with Him for deliverance. If this was *His* venture, as they believed, would *He* not now deliver them? They *hoped* (for in their weakened state, the word *believed* might be too strong to use) He would. And–*He DID!*

In the middle of March, on a fair day, suddenly they were alerted by their guard that an Indian was coming–a *lone* Indian. As they looked toward the woods, they saw a tall Indian striding toward their "fort-meeting house" (as they called their church building). He walked up to them and stated, "Welcome Englishmen!" They couldn't believe what they were hearing. A *friendly* Indian, who spoke *English*! They were amazed!

He was a chief from up in Maine who was visiting the region that winter, evidently for no other purpose than the fact that he liked to sightsee. Samoset, as their guest identified himself, had learned his broken English from sea captains who had put into his waters from time to time to fish. He had hitched a ride with one of these captains down the coast to Plymouth, and had been staying with the nearest *sachem,* or chief, who ruled loosely over the tribes around the Cape. After he had spent the night with them (under the watchful eye of Captain Standish's guard), he promised them he would bring to them in a few days another Indian who spoke better English than he.

No doubt they watched in bewilderment as their newfound friend faded into the woods. They hardly knew what to make of it. Was he for real? Could they trust him? While these questions remained unanswered, they were hardly in a position to refuse friendship when extended to them. They could only hope he was on the level. In the meantime, there was work to do.

Sure enough, about a week later, Samoset showed up again. This time he brought with him the other Indian he had promised to introduce to them. This man's name was Tisquantum, which the Pilgrims would shorten to Squanto. He did speak their language very well. And his story was hard to believe. If we knew all the details, it could easily fill a large volume.

Squanto had grown up on this very ground where they were now living. His tribe, the Pautauxets, were the ones who had tilled this soil. They also had been the most war-like tribe on the Cape, killing every white man they possibly could. But where were they now? He told the Pilgrims they were all dead. About four years before, an unexplainable disease had come among them and killed every man, woman, and child. It was for this reason the other Indians on the Cape had not attacked them here. The local tribes believed it was an evil spirit that had brought this awful plague, and they were afraid to come near this place.

Though awed by this Providential occurrence, the Pilgrims still had questions. One was, if all this was true, why was *he* still alive? What he told them was one of the most amazing stories, (and they believed–*acts of Providence*) in all of history.

As a young brave, Squanto and some of his friends had been lured onto a ship by a captain who pretended to want to trade with them. Once aboard, this wicked captain, Hunt by name, had his sailors wrestle the lads into irons. Their intended destination: the slave block in the ports of Spain!

Somehow though–and the Pilgrims always believed it was the Providential Hand of God–Squanto managed to escape from Captain Hunt and made his way to England. There, he was befriended by an English merchant. This businessman gave him work and taught him the English language. He was there a number of years and had managed to get back to his homeland only a few months before the Pilgrims arrived.

The Pilgrims must have been "blown away" by this whole story. To think how God had protected and prepared this man, who was to become "a special instrument sent of God for their good,"[5] was astounding. If they, themselves, had planned for someone to help them in this wilderness, they couldn't have done nearly as well. They were overwhelmed with the sense of God's Providential care. His thoughts of them who were committed to Him had, indeed, been "more than the sands of the seashore."[6]

Squanto settled right in; and he never left. He would live with the Pilgrims until the day he died. He did become "a special instrument sent of God for their good."[7] He taught them how to hunt and fish successfully in this wilderness. He taught them how to plant corn, which would be their main staple in the early years. He taught them how to trap the beaver, the pelts of which would bring a great price in Europe. This became the primary way they paid their debts to the businessmen who had financed their trip.

But perhaps the most important thing Squanto did for them was to help them enter into a peace treaty with Chief Massasoit, who, as already mentioned, was the leading chief in that region. That treaty was of great mutual benefit to the Pilgrims and to Masssasoit's tribe. And, contrary to what we often hear of our ancestors' early relations with the natives of America, it lasted for over 50 years. Indeed, when it finally was broken, it was Massasoit's son, known as King Phillip, who broke it.

"So," you ask, "what did the Pilgrims do for Squanto?" They did the two most important things you can ever do for anyone. First, they became his family: That remarkable group God created to help us become all He made us to be–*family*. The Pilgrims loved and cared for Squanto as long as they knew him, though that time was quite short. Secondly, they did the greatest thing for him any human being could do for another. By their example and their words, they shared with him who Jesus Christ was. Having been introduced to Christ, when the moment of death came for Squanto, he asked Governor Bradford to pray for him, "that he might go to the Englishmen's God in heaven."[8] Thus, they had begun to fulfill their vision of "...propagating the Gospel of Christ in those remote parts of the world." It would seem Squanto was the beneficiary of that greatest of all gifts, "eternal life."

Looking back, several questions arrest our attention. What if the storms had not blown the Pilgrims off course *and* into Plymouth Bay? What if the Patauxets had still been alive when the Pilgrims did find Plymouth? What if Squanto had not been captured and taken to England and prepared there to live with the Pilgrims by learning their language and customs? What if Samoset had not gone "sightseeing" that winter of 1620-21? While those questions can't be answered, it does become obvious that the Providence of God was at work, preparing both a place and knowledge by which the Pilgrims would be provided for in this new land: This land where a person would have the right to believe in Christ as the Redeemer; this land where one could receive that Christ right into himself, and then allow Christ to live His life through him in this world, thus enabling a person to become all God had created him to be. This would be a land where He would establish liberty for the Gospel to go to the next generation!

Late that fall in 1621, Governor Bradford issued a proclamation setting aside a special day in which the community was to assemble at the "fort-meeting house" and give thanks to God for protecting and providing for them in this new land. That summer had produced a sufficient crop to get them through the winter until spring, when the game would again be plentiful. For this harvest they were very grateful.

Since Chief Massasoit had been such a friend to them, they invited him to come to the special occasion also. Little did they know that Massasoit would take the invitation to mean his whole tribe. When he showed up with his chief wives and 90 braves, the Pilgrims must have swallowed hard. To feed this crowd would wipe out much of their food stored for the winter. What were they to do?

They did what they always (at least *eventually*) did. They decided to "give to him who asks of you."[9] As it turned out, the Lord already had provision. Massasoit had told his braves to hunt so they could take meat to the feast. They came with five dressed deer and a number of wild turkeys. It was a feast they would all remember.

After the meals, the young men competed in wrestling matches and foot races. The Indians loved this and wanted more of it. In fact, the Indians stayed for *three* days! The Pilgrims, not wanting to offend their friends, agreed to extend the feast. It was a joyous occasion for all.

The high point of the celebration had to be when their Pastor, William Brewster, prayed at the beginning of the first meal. With the waves lapping against the shore of Plymouth Bay, he began to lift his voice to God, in the Name of Jesus Christ. His heart was full. As he considered the provision and the protection of their Heavenly Father, he began to express their heartfelt gratitude to God. There was the food He had provided; the shelter He had enabled them to build–some of it the previous winter in the most difficult weather conditions. Then there was Squanto who had been such a help to them, along with Samoset being there in the "right place at the right time" to connect them with Squanto. Also, their friendship with Massasoit was such a miracle! Probably no other chief on the New England coast would have ever considered an alliance with "outsiders." And then, there were those the Lord had called away through death the previous winter. Their memory was precious to them. But even more important was the fact that there was a heaven God had provided for them to go to: A place where all suffering ceases, and all wrong is righted!

It *was indeed* a memorable occasion. So much so that it would begin a tradition in America that has been carried on ever since. How much we have to be grateful for, when we consider the Pilgrims and their sacrifice on our behalf! What lives they lived! What lives of devotion to Jesus Christ, allowing Him to literally live His life through them.

The Pilgrims would have many more trials in the settling of this new land. But no other time would be as hard as that first winter had been. And, thanks to God's Providential Hand, working with and through the sacrifice of those committed to Him, the truth of the Gospel of Christ's Kingdom was taking deeper root in the "new world!" There would now be a nation in which a person could allow Jesus Christ to live His life through him without fear of religious, governmental, or economic persecution. And while America would not be heaven, *it would be free!*

The Pilgrims created a community which would become the seed of the greatest nation in world history. They allowed more liberty for more individuals than any nation of their day.

Likewise, they created cultural institutions of education, economy, and government. They learned both the "form and the spirit" of those institutions in the Bible. Thus, they literally created the seed of a nation based on the Bible. That was why Andrew Jackson would later say to a group of men, "That Book, Gentlemen, is the rock on which this Republic rests."[10]

This tiny group, consisting of common men, created what would become *the greatest nation in history*. How did they do it?

First, they came to believe, while still in England, that God *was*, and that He had a good plan for each individual He would create on this earth. They became "enlightened by the Word of God and had their ignorance and sins discovered unto them," as Bradford would put it.[11] In other words, they learned that man had rebelled against the plan of God to live inside him and express His life through him. But, they also had revealed to them that God had sent Jesus to live a sinless life, then offer that life up to God at the Cross, to pay our debt so that we might be "reconciled to God."[12] They likewise came to believe that Jesus had been raised from the dead so that He could now take up residence inside anyone who would believe in Him.[13] They had repented and agreed with God that their lives were not actually theirs, but His.[14] They had acknowledged His right to rule them, and to rule *through them*, in this world.

Secondly, through their experiences in England and Holland, including their exposure to the teaching of the Reformation Fathers like Wycliffe and Calvin, they became convinced that part of the "ruling" God wanted to do through them was in the cultural institutions of *education, government*, and *economy*. As they searched the Scriptures, they came to realize *it was God* Who had the better plan for these institutions; and that, if we would work with Him, He would establish those institutions in a way which would promote the truth (the Gospel of the Kingdom of Christ) going to the next generation. That became *their* dream; and it has ever been the *only true American dream!*

So they established an **educational system** which would teach the Gospel of Christ–and every *academic* subject from the principles of that Gospel!

They, in 1623, established an **economic system** based on the Biblical principle of private ownership. Today we call that system *free enterprise*. In other words, the government has no right to interfere in the market place! They believed this economic system would prosper them enough to be able to operate their educational system successfully. They were right.

They created, as their form of **government**, a ***Biblical Republic.*** That is, a government in which law, based on the Bible, was the highest authority. Also, that law must be chosen by the vote of the people through their elected representatives. This *Republic* would *protect* their *educational* and *economic* institutions so their children could hear and have opportunity to walk in *the Gospel of Jesus Christ,* thus fulfilling the plan of God for their lives.[15]

The rest is history. Simply put: Jesus Christ flowed through these early American believers, and through the cultural institutions they created. And while that flow was not perfect (since the Pilgrims were humans), it was consistent. The result: The greatest nation the world has ever seen was created. This is the simple truth of what made America great. ***It is all that gives it worth today!***

Chapter 15

Codifying the Pilgrim Vision Into Law

In the hot summer of 1776, a group of 56 delegates gathered in Philadelphia to discuss their differences with the British Crown and Parliament. The most important question to be decided was: Who was the source of their rights of life, liberty, and property? Was the source *God* or *government?*

England thought the colonies existed for the good of the Mother country. Thus, they thought the rights of the colonists were *"government granted."* The people in America thought they existed for the *"glory of God and the advancement of the Christian faith,"* as the Pilgrims had stated in the Mayflower Compact. Thus, Americans believed that their rights were *"God granted."*

What must be decided was: Is Parliament and the English King the highest authority, or is there a higher law in place? If there was a higher law, did the colonists have to submit to laws that disagreed with that higher law?

The Americans did believe there was a higher law, which was the Law of God written in the Bible. The ministers of this time period in America were remarkably agreed on this position. They quoted over and over the passage in Romans 13:1-2 which states:

> *"Let every soul be subject to the higher powers. For there is no power but of God; the powers that be are ordained of God. Whosoever therefore resists the power, resists the ordinance of God…."*

The people of the American colonies believed the English King had violated the rights of their original documents (called Charters) which guaranteed their right of self-government. They believed self-government was a Biblical right. Americans believed their charters had given them equal rights as British citizens to make their own laws, so long as those laws agreed with the English Constitution. No tax or regulation could be put on them without violating this British Constitution. And the British government had generally accepted this as their right for nearly 150 years.

But now the English government was trying to change the original agreement within those charters _without_ the approval of the colonists' representatives. And, in August of 1775, the King had even _removed_ their right to make their own laws by _canceling_ their colonial legislatures! (As if he had that right!) At the same time, he and the English Parliament were forcing laws _on_ the colonies without any approval _from_ the colonies.

The American colonists had always viewed themselves as citizens of Great Britain, having the same rights as any Englishman who lived within the British Isles. But now their rights were being denied. If they submitted to this violation of their Charters, their right to the protection of their life, liberty, and property would be gone. They would be living under complete tyranny. To accept such tyranny would be to violate their own conscience, as well as to ignore the sacrifice of their forefathers in planting liberty on these shores.

And in addition to this, because the English king and Parliament were making laws without the authority of the people who were affected by those laws, the British officials had moved out from under the lawful flow of God's authority. This meant that if the Americans were to obey the law of Parliament, they would be disobeying the law of God. _They, themselves,_ would then be out of God's order, and thus the flow of His blessing. This they could never do!

Colonial Pastors had, for many years, taught their congregations that resistance to tyranny is obedience to God. This was echoed in the Massachusetts Provincial Congress in 1774. The delegates stated:

> "Resistance to tyranny becomes the Christian and social
> duty of each individual....Continue steadfast and, with a
> proper sense of your dependence on God, nobly defend

101

those rights which heaven gave, and no man ought to take from us."[1]

In April of 1775, Americans had already spilled their blood at Lexington and Concord resisting the tyrannical actions of the British government and its army of "Redcoats." Now they must consider if a final break with the Mother country was necessary in order to re-establish *God-given* governmental authority.

To the men gathered in Philadelphia, this decision was every bit as heart-rending as it was difficult to implement. The delegates from the colonies had begun these Continental Congresses on their knees, crying to the God of heaven for both the courage to do what was right, as well as the strength to face an overwhelming army in a war that would surely come. They had knelt, signifying that their rights came from God and that they were appealing to Him to show that their cause was just. They were declaring their *dependence* on Him before they ever declared their *independence* from England.

It was in this spirit that Virginia delegate, Richard Henry Lee, would propose the resolution on June 7th that "these colonies are, and of right ought to be, free and independent states."[2] A committee would shortly be appointed to draft a *Declaration of Independence*. Thomas Jefferson would do most of the writing of that *Declaration,* in which he would declare the reason that caused the separation:

> "...We hold these truths to be self-evident, that all men are created equal, that they are endowed by their Creator with certain unalienable rights; that among these are life, liberty, and the pursuit of happiness; that to secure these rights, governments are instituted among men, deriving their just powers from the consent of the governed; <u>that whenever any form of government becomes destructive of these ends, it is the right of the people to alter or to abolish it, and to institute new government...</u>"
> (emphasis added)

The *Declaration* would be presented to the Continental Congress on Monday, July 1st, after a three week recess had given the delegates time to once again consider the full implications of separating from England.

Even so, they hesitated to make the break. Dickinson from Pennsylvania spoke against independence in his very eloquent way. A long silence ensued after he sat down. The destiny of future generations hung in the balance. Slowly, John Adams arose to his feet to speak, for what seemed to him to be one more time added to too many already. He spoke quietly, but with great conviction and emotion:

"Before God, I believe the hour has come. My judgment approves this measure, and my whole heart is in it. All that I have, and all that I am, and all that I hope in this life, I am now ready here to stake upon it. And I leave off as I began, that live or die, survive or perish, I am for the Declaration. It is my living sentiment, and by the blessing of God it shall be my dying sentiment. Independence now, and Independence forever!"[3]

What would the delegates do? Even with Adams' moving appeal, they still hesitated to approve the *Declaration*. Would sentimental ties with England, or the fear of the devastation of war, keep them from standing with the order of God? Would they, as Patrick Henry had warned, hang on to "peace…at the price of chains and slavery"?[4]

Finally, John Witherspoon, a new delegate now representing New Jersey, arose to his feet. Though unknown to our generation, here was a man greatly respected by our Founding generation. Like Patrick Henry, he was of Scotch descent, and had inherited the love of liberty from his ancestors, who had fought English tyranny for hundreds of years. A very scholarly minister, he was now the President of Princeton College (present day Princeton University). He was known as the "man who shaped the men who shaped America."[5] He had trained many of our Founders, and he loved liberty more than life. Though new to the convention, he took to the floor in that moment of hesitation and spoke with fiery boldness of the "colonies [being] ripe for independence."[6] His fervency and boldness won the day. When the vote was taken, independence had won!

Their commitment to the cause of re-establishing Godly government was real. They closed the *Declaration* by saying,

> *"And for the support of this Declaration, with a firm reliance on the protection of Divine Providence, we mutually pledge to each other our lives, our fortunes, and our sacred honor."*

Many would lose their fortunes; some would lose their lives; but NONE would lose their sacred honor because ALL kept their pledge!

By miracles in the war to follow, that Godly government was re-established. And over the next eleven years, they would work with that government to make it better: And the end product, our national *Constitution* (written in 1787 and approved by the states by 1789), was no less a miracle. Many of our Founders would speak of the miracle that brought our national *Constitution* into being. George Washington would acknowledge God's hand in that Constitutional Convention in a letter to his good friend, Jonathan Trumbull, then Governor of Connecticut:

> *"...we may, with a kind of pious and grateful exultation, trace the Finger of Providence through those dark and mysterious events which first induced the States to appoint a general Convention, and then led them one after another...to effect the...adoption of the system recommended by that general Convention; thereby in all human probability laying a lasting foundation for tranquillity and happiness...*

"That the same Good Providence may still continue to protect us, and prevent us from dashing the cup on national felicity, just as it has been lifted to our lips, is [my] earnest prayer..."[7]

James Madison, who was the chief author of our national *Constitution,* likewise acknowledged the blessing and protection of God in bringing forth this new government.

"No people ought to feel greater obligations to celebrate the goodness of the Great Disposer...of the Destiny of Nations than the people of the United States. His kind providence originally conducted them to one of the best portions of the dwelling place allotted for the great family of the human race. He protected and cherished them under all the difficulties and trials to which they were exposed in their early days. Under His fostering care, their habits...prepared them for a transition in due time to a state of independence and self-government. In the arduous struggle by which it was attained they were distinguished by multiplied tokens of His benign interposition. During the interval which succeeded He reared them into the strength and endowed them with the resources which have enabled them to assert their national rights..."[8]

Now at last, the Pilgrim vision of creating government that would protect the right to take the Gospel of the Kingdom of Christ to the next generation was done on a national level, just as it had already been done on a state level. As all law is just the codification of some religious belief, the religious beliefs of the Pilgrims had now grown from internal self-government all the way to the external civil government, even at a national level.

All that was left was for the message of the Gospel of the Kingdom of Christ to go to each succeeding generation, that they might have the opportunity to choose to let Jesus Christ come into their life, and flow through them to *their children*. Thus, they would become "a vessel fit for the master's use"[9] in their spirit, soul, and body: Individuals, and a generation, through which God could live His life!

Americans would now be free to make that choice, both as individuals and as a nation.

Epilogue:

Our Choice: Repentance or Destruction

America's founding documents, *The Declaration of Independence* and *The Constitution,* had codified into law the Pilgrim vision. Those documents had created a national government that agreed with already established colonial governments. These governments all protected the right of Biblical *education* and Biblical *economy* (*Free Enterprise*). *Because* these institutions, and the spirit they operated in, *were* Biblically based, America grew to be the most free and prosperous nation in world history. This was exactly what God promised in Deuteronomy 28. He had said:

> "...If you will diligently obey the voice of the Lord your God, to observe carefully all His commandments...the Lord your God will set you high above all nations of the earth...The Lord will command the blessing on you in your storehouses and all to which you set your hand, and He will bless you in the land which the Lord your God is giving you. The Lord will establish you as a holy people to Himself...if you keep the commandments of the Lord your God and walk in His ways. Then all peoples of the earth shall see that you are called by the name of the Lord...The Lord will make you the head and not the tail, you shall be above only, and not beneath, if you heed the commandments of the Lord your God..." (vv. 1-13)

The Bible is true and works in this present world. The Founding Fathers of America proved this. Neither were they hesitant in expressing this. They wanted their children to understand where this nation, that was becoming the envy of the world, came from.

In 1820, Daniel Webster, while dedicating Plymouth Rock (our first national monument), identified the source of America's institutions when he stated:

"Our ancestors established their system of government on morality and religious sentiment...a government and a country were to commence with the very first foundations laid under the divine light of the Christian religion...Let us not forget the religious character of our origin. Our fathers were brought [here] by their high [respect] for the Christian religion. They journeyed by its light and labored in its hope. They sought to...diffuse its influence through all their institutions, civil, political, or [educational]."[1]

Noah Webster, the Father of America's original educational methodology, revealed:

"The religion which has introduced civil liberty is the religion of Christ and His apostles...This is genuine Christianity and to it we owe our free constitutions of government."[2]

John Quincy Adams, our sixth President and son of Founder, John Adams, described what the American Revolution accomplished. He stated:

"The highest glory of the American Revolution was this, it connected in one indissoluble bond, the principles of civil government with the principles of Christianity."[3]

John Adams, 2nd President and also a signer of the Declaration of Independence, summed up the view of most of our Founders concerning the birthing of America when he stated these words:

"I always consider the settlement of America with reverence and wonder, as the opening of a grand...design in Providence for the illumination of the ignorant, and the emancipation of the slavish part of mankind all over the earth."[4]

These, along with thousands of other recorded statements, reveal the faith of our Founding Fathers. Their commitment was to Jesus Christ. Their wisdom was gained from the Bible. While not perfect, as no human is (including their critics!), they did make diligent efforts to live and build their nation by the principles of the Bible.

We would do well to return to their example.

Not until the early 1900's, when some began a calculated effort to remove from America those Biblical principles, did we start the downhill trend that has grown more rapid ever since. Because we, who are Christians, backed out of the culture in the early 1900's, we allowed the humanist takeover now so prevalent in our nation. With the passing of each day, we are more and more reaping the fruit of man-centered ideas. The breakdown of the traditional home, the enslavement of so many to drugs, materialism, and the lust for pleasure threatens our very existence. Without a return to the Biblical principles of our Founders, the loss of our liberty is *certain!*

In that same Bible passage in Deuteronomy 28, which promises such blessing for *obedience*, is the strong warning that *disobedience* will bring disaster. In verse 15 God warns:

"But it shall come to pass, if you do not obey the voice of the LORD your God, to observe carefully all His commandments and His statutes which I command you today, that all these curses will come upon you and overtake you..."You shall betroth a wife, but another man shall lie with her (consider the tremendous breakdown of the family we now have); *you shall build a house, but you*

shall not dwell in it (note the great rise in bankruptcies in recent years)...*⁵"The alien who is among you shall rise higher and higher above you, and you shall come down lower and lower. ⁶He shall lend to you, but you shall not lend to him* (consider how many of our banks are now owned by Arabs, Japanese, or other foreign investors)*; he shall be the head, and you shall be the tail." (Deuteronomy 28: 15,30,43,44)*

Friend, God is serious about His Word! The disintegration of American culture is everywhere evident to those who have the discernment and courage to admit it. We have, since the 1960's, experienced ever-increasing waves of moral breakdown, bringing us even to the point that we would murder our own children by abortion (Fifty million since 1973!), and accept homosexuality as normal. We are, more and more, experiencing the dreaded curses written in Deuteronomy 28, as well as many other Biblical passages.

But God does not delight in the death of something He's created, individual or national; and He *did* create America. He says in Acts 17:26,

"For [God] has made of one blood every <u>nation</u> of men to dwell on all the face of the earth...and has determined their boundaries..." (emphasis added)

God created America to raise up a nation which would protect, by law, a person's right to allow Him to live His life through him; and which would, through its educational system and economic system, communicate to the next generation that purpose. He does not delight in seeing its death by the poison of anti-God philosophy. He is, even yet, extending His offer of mercy and restoration to us. He says,

"...if My people who are called by My name will humble themselves, and pray and seek My face, and turn from

their wicked ways, <u>then I will</u> hear from heaven, and will forgive their sin and heal their land." (2 Chronicles 7:14) (emphasis added)

In the past, revival has saved other nations, as well as our own. The fresh wind of God breathing new life into individuals, families, churches, communities, and regions can save us from our own destruction. We have examples of this in the past.

In the 1730's John and Charles Wesley and their followers began to "salt down" England with short portions of the Bible and their comments on the need for England and her people to turn back to the God of their birth. Terrible decay had set into English society. People were living for pleasure instead of purpose. By neglect, children were being denied the opportunity to hear the Gospel of the Kingdom of Christ, and thus were growing up to be like their parents. It seemed deeper and deeper depravity was all the future held.

Into this darkness the Wesleys began to introduce the light of the Gospel of Christ, calling on men to acknowledge that their lives were the rightful property of the God Who created them. Young people began to see the truth and respond to it. As more and more repented and turned to Christ as their personal Master, the light grew, and with it the exposure of sin in the culture. And, as truth always does when given the right to be heard, it began to change the society. As men, women, and young people turned more and more to Christ as Lord, their Godly lives began to be felt. At first gradually, then more and more, sin and its death was driven from the nation; first by individual choices, then by civil laws that reflected the Godly choices of growing masses of people.

As a fruit of this growing movement, slavery would be abolished in England (1833) by the persistent efforts of one William Wilberforce. The Awakening in England made such an impact on the whole society that even Lecky, a secular historian, admitted it saved civilization in England.[5]

Likewise revival has, more than once, saved America from destruction. As with England, revival also came to America in the

1730's. This fresh breath from the Spirit of God would wash over the American colonies repeatedly, with varying intensity, for the next 30 years. The churches were brought to a deeper walk with Christ as individuals repented of sin and let that repentance affect their families and communities.

It started in 1734 in a little village on the frontier of Massachusetts called North Hampton.

A Godly Pastor, Jonathan Edwards, preached the Scriptural warnings about self-centeredness and its results being a hell of fire in eternity, as well as destruction in this life. The Holy Spirit came in such power that Sunday morning that grown men who were hardened sinners grabbed for the posts holding up the roof of the church because they felt themselves physically slipping into hell! The spiritual fire spread to other communities as people came to North Hampton and experienced the work of God's fresh wind. As they returned with repentant hearts to their communities and told the story of what they'd experienced, the "fire of God" would fall on their communities as well.

Before many months, all the American colonies were caught up in a move of God that would sweep an estimated 75% of the 3 million Americans on this continent into the Kingdom of God. It would affect society at all levels and instill Biblical thinking into America's Founders (all of whom were born during or just before this period). Educational, economic, and governmental practices were all profoundly affected by the renewal in Biblical thinking that occurred.

Ben Franklin was greatly impressed by what he was seeing happen in Philadelphia during this revival period. He revealed how it changed that city:

> *"It was wonderful to see the change soon made in the manners of our inhabitants. From being thoughtless or indifferent about religion, it seemed as if all the world were growing religious, so that one could not walk thro' the town in an evening without hearing psalms sung in different families of every street."*[6]

This revival not only saved America from the destruction of selfishness, it also shaped the thinking of our Founding Fathers so that they were able to reason from the Bible all the governmental principles of our *Declaration of Independence* and our *Constitution*. It was the principle of "sowing and reaping," they gleaned from the Bible, that enabled them to see far into the future the results that a certain governmental action would produce. These ideas founded in the Scripture gave us the stability of our system, and has made America the oldest living Republic in world history!

All this stability is rooted in the Biblical thinking produced by this *Great Awakening* (as it came to be called) toward God and His Word. *We owe our very liberty to God and His Word!*

By 1825, the children and grandchildren of those touched by the *Great Awakening* were in need of another move of God. In answer to the prayers of discerning believers, God began to move through an individual we might consider very unlikely to be used of God, since he was a lawyer. However, the attorneys of that day had one very great advantage over the lawyers of our day. They were trained in the study of law, primarily, with Blackstone's *Commentaries on the Law*. William Blackstone had published these *Commentaries* in 1765, and had stated in them what he believed the foundation of all civil law should be. He wrote:

"The [teaching] thus delivered we call the revealed...law, and they are to be found only in the Holy Scriptures...no human law should be [allowed] to contradict these."[7]

It was these Biblically based commentaries on the law which were to be used to bring attorney Charles Finney, to repentance and faith in Jesus Christ as His own personal Lord.

He would be the instrument in God's hand which would call whole regions of America back to God.

His method was to go into a community and begin to preach on the Law of God summarized in the Ten Commandments until the people either repented for breaking that law–or they ran the lawyer out of town. He reasoned, from the pulpit, with people about their sin, the same way he would have presented a case in the courtroom. Because the Holy Spirit was present due to the prayers of humble saints, thousands were powerfully affected by his preaching.

Through Finey's ministry in Rochester, N.Y., in the late 1820's, God came in such a way that the whole city was changed. An eye-witness would write:

"The whole community was stirred. Religion was the topic of conversation, in the house, in the shop, in the office and on the street...The only theater in the city was converted into a livery stable; the only circus into a soap and candle factory. [Bars] were closed; the Sabbath was honored; the sanctuaries were thronged with happy worshippers...the fountains of benevolence were opened, and men lived to do good..."

"It is not too much to say that the whole character of the city was changed by that revival. Most of the leaders of society being converted, and exerting a controlling influence in social life, in business, and in civil affairs, religion was enthroned as it has been in few places...Even the courts and the prisons bore witness to its blessed effects. There was a wonderful falling off in crime. The courts had little to do, and the jail was nearly empty for years afterward."[8]

Can this kind of revival happen again? Absolutely! Is God the "same yesterday, today, and forever?"[9] I cannot help but believe if God has withheld final judgment from us after thirty-five years of us killing our own children through abortion–if He's spared us that long when we deserve to be judged–I can only conclude it's for the purpose of granting us revival. The "ball is in our court," so to speak.

What can we do (Perhaps it's better said, what *must* we do!) in order for our children to live in liberty? We must accept that the responsibility is *ours*. _We_ will make the difference, if there is a difference made. The people of God are the *only* hope in this nation. The secular humanists are deceived and have no clue that they are leading us toward destruction. We who are "born again," and thus make up the church of Jesus Christ, must accept our responsibility to be "salt and light" in this culture. God wants to flow through us to this decadent society. He wants to share both a *word of righteousness* to re-establish His moral standard, and a *word of hope* that those enslaved to ungodly ideas can be freed to become a vessel of God's life in this earth!

To be more specific:

First, we need to *acknowledge* that Jesus Christ has the exclusive rights to this life which we have called "our own." He created us and redeemed us, and therefore we are rightfully His, not our own. He created us "in His image, after His likeness"[10] so we could be a carrier of His life in this world; so He could express Himself through us. He died on a Roman cross, and rose from the dead so He could restore us to God, which makes possible His coming to live inside us, that He might live *through us in this present culture!* He makes this plain in 1 Corinthians 6:19-20 when He says,

> "...*you are not your own...you were bought with a price; therefore glorify God in your body and in your spirit, which are God's.*"

You must admit it: You're *His–not yours!*

Secondly, you and I must *repent* of (change our minds about) receiving anti-God philosophy. Whether we got it from our parents, the secular school system (including the universities), the music we're listening to, the news media, or somewhere else, we need to change our minds and admit that it disagrees with God's way of thinking revealed in the Bible. *Repentance* means we turn from it; we stop listening to it and begin to seek the truth; for Jesus taught that only "...the truth will make you free."[11]

Thirdly, if you haven't yet received Christ as your personal Lord, earnestly ask Him to, right now, enter your life and become your *Master and Deliverer.* If you already know Christ, surrender *afresh* every area of life to Him, confessing every known sin to Him, one by one. If those sins involve others, confess them to those people too. Confession should be as broad as the sin is known. (A few individuals knowing it means confessing it to each of them individually; if it's broadly known, then going in front of a church, which teaches the Bible to be completely true, is perhaps the best way to admit your sin.) God promises, "If we confess our sins, He is faithful and just to forgive us our sins, and to cleanse us from all unrighteousness."[12] Similarly, the Bible admonishes us, "Whosoever covers his sin will not prosper, but he who confesses and forsakes it will have mercy." [13]

Fourthly–*and this cannot be emphasized too strongly!*–begin to read the Bible, *and read it through!* If you're in the habit of daily reading it, start now to read it from Genesis to Revelation, and make that your normal practice for the rest of your life. If you haven't read it much, then start by reading the Gospel of John, then read the New Testament through, maybe several times. Thereafter, read Genesis through Revelation, as already described. The reason for this is that we only get God's mind if we read the Bible.[14] And we won't get His whole mind (I speak of knowing what He wants us to know about life in *this* world) unless we read it through. So much of His teaching about the institutions of the culture (education, economy, and government) are written in little known parts of the Bible–at least they are little known to most of us. We must begin again to read it completely through so as to not miss His all-important teaching about the cultural institutions.

America's Founders got their wisdom from the Bible. One study revealed that of all their speeches and writings, if they quoted an outside source, over 33% of the time they quoted the Bible: And 60% of the remainder of the time, they taught *principles gleaned from the Bible!*[15] Is it now clear why they were able to create the greatest nation in world history? It should be! *And,* if they achieved such a monumental thing with the wisdom they received from Scripture, shouldn't you and I be reading it through on a daily basis? Indeed, many of them actually identified, as their method of Bible reading, that they read it through from year to year. We know, from entries in his journal, that John Quincy Adams read it through *at least 55 times!* I believe with everything that's in me, if American liberty is to be preserved so the Gospel of the Kingdom of Christ can go to the next generation, it will be because we return to reading the Bible through–learning and obeying its teachings. Presently, we are not teaching it simply because we don't know it ourselves; and you can no more teach what you don't know, that you can come back from somewhere you've never been. We simply *must return to reading the Scripture completely through!*

Lastly, to see the liberty of your children preserved so they can hear and walk in the Gospel of Jesus Christ, we must do something else. We must rediscover our Founder's writings. Because they already reasoned educational, economic, and governmental principles from the Bible, we can glean from their understanding and not have to "re-invent the wheel." Not that we elevate their thoughts to be equal with the Bible; rather, we will learn, by reading their writings, that they tried to *submit* their thoughts *to the Bible*, and that's why they were generally right about what they wrote. America's Founders' wisdom has been purposely hidden from our children by humanists for almost *four generations!* The demise of our nation is the convicting testimony that we lack our Founders' Biblical wisdom. (You may be wondering where you can find the Founders' writings. I will list a few of them for your convenience in the *addendum* following this epilogue.)

How seriously should we take the cultural signs of destruction which surround us?

Peter Marshall, Chaplain of the United States Senate in 1947 (a time when humanists were highly optimistic about the world they were creating) stated penetrating words. He said,

"The choice before us is plain: Christ or chaos, conviction or compromise, discipline or disintegration. I am rather tired of

117

*hearing about our rights and privileges as American citizens. The time is come - it is now - when we ought to hear about the duties and responsibilities of our citizenship. **America's future depends upon her accepting and demonstrating God's government.**"[16]* (emphasis added)

Is there hope that God will revive and restore this nation? In the darkest days of the 1800's, during the War Between the States, Abraham Lincoln echoed deep Biblical principles when he wrote the *Proclamation Appointing a National Fast Day,* for the purpose of calling the nation to repentance.

Consider carefully these wise words revealing, not only Lincoln's deep burden and hope, but the very heart of God. Lincoln wrote:

"Whereas, the Senate of the United States devoutly recognizing the Supreme Authority and just Government of Almighty God in all the affairs of men and of nations, has, by a resolution, requested the President to designate and set apart a day for national prayer and humiliation; and

Whereas, it is the duty of nations as well as of men to own their dependence upon the overruling power of God, to confess their sins and transgressions in humble sorrow yet with assured hope that genuine repentance will lead to mercy and pardon, and to recognize the sublime truth, announced in the Holy Scriptures and proven by all history: that those nations only are blessed whose God is the Lord;

And, insomuch as we know that, by His divine law, nations like individuals are subjected to punishments and chastisement in this world, may we not justly fear that the awful calamity of civil war, which now desolates the land may be but a punishment inflicted upon us for our presumptuous sins to the needful end of our national reformation as a whole people?

We have been the recipients of the choicest bounties of Heaven. We have been preserved these many years in peace and prosperity. We have grown in numbers, wealth and power as no other nation has ever grown.

But we have forgotten God. We have forgotten the gracious Hand which preserved us in peace, and multiplied and enriched and strengthened us; and we have vainly imagined, in the deceitfulness of our hearts, that all these blessings were produced by some superior wisdom and virtue of our own.

Intoxicated with unbroken success, we have become too self-sufficient to feel the necessity of redeeming and preserving grace, too proud to pray to the God that made us!

It behooves us then to humble ourselves before the offended Power, to confess our national sins and to pray for clemency and forgiveness.

Now, therefore, in compliance with the request and fully concurring in the view of the Senate, I do, by this my proclamation, designate and set apart Thursday, the 30th day of April, 1863, as a day of national humiliation, fasting and prayer.

And I do hereby request all the people to abstain on that day from their ordinary secular pursuits, and to unite, at their several places of public worship and their respective homes, in keeping the day holy to the Lord and devoted to the humble discharge of the religious duties proper to that solemn occasion.

All this being done, in sincerity and truth, let us then rest humbly in the hope authorized by the Divine teachings, that the united cry of the nation will be heard on high and answered with blessing no less than the pardon of our national sins and the restoration of our now divided and suffering country to its former happy condition of unity and peace.

In witness whereof, I have hereunto set my hand and caused the seal of the United States to be affixed. Done at the city of Washington, this 30th day of March, A.D. 1863, and of the Independence of the United States the eighty-seventh.

(Signed)

Abraham Lincoln.[17]

This *Proclamation* was written the end of March, 1863. The Battle of Gettysburg was fought less than four months later. That battle would turn the war in favor of the Northern forces. God obviously honored their repentance.

We may gain further hope from more words of wisdom from "Kentucky's Favorite Son," spoken just a few days before the Battle of Gettysburg. Replying to a college President who asked him if he thought the country would survive, Lincoln stated,

> "I do not doubt that our country will finally come through safe and undivided. But do not misunderstand me....I do not rely on the patriotism of our people...the bravery and devotion of the boys in blue...(or) the loyalty and skill of our generals....
>
> "But the God of our fathers, who raised up this country to be the refuge and asylum of the oppressed and downtrodden of all nations, will not let it perish now. I may not live to see it...I do not expect to see it, but God will bring us through safe."[18]

In conclusion, let me say once more, the deciding question is: Will you and I, as individuals, allow the Christ Who created us to be the complete Master of every area of our lives? Will we acknowledge His *right* and His *ability* to be in us and through us all He created us to be. Will we, once again, believe that His way works _in this present world_? That is what *revival* is. That is what it has always been.

Consider Harriet Beecher Stowe's final words in her book, *Uncle Tom's Cabin*, the book that was one of the main reasons the War Between the States occurred:

> *"A day of grace is yet held out to us. Both North and South have been guilty before God; and the Christian church has a heavy account to answer. Not by combining together, to protect injustice and cruelty, and making a*

common capital of sin, is this Union to be saved, but by repentance, justice and mercy."[19]

There are some signs that revival may be beginning in our land: The growing movement among college age adults to live out a total commitment to Jesus Christ is one sign. Another is the growing participation by Godly citizens in the operations of their governments. Most encouraging is the increasing number of prayer groups, who's only reason to meet, is to pray for revival in our land. A number of those meetings are occurring right here in our region. Surely these are signs from the Lord to encourage us that *revival is possible*, if we will join our fellow Americans in these movements.

May God help us to return to Him, allowing Him to create the same testimony in us, by which the Apostle Paul lived:

"I have been crucified with Christ, nevertheless I live, yet not I, but Christ liveth in me. And the life I now live in the flesh, I live by the faith of the Son of God Who loved me and gave Himself for me."[20]

<u>This</u> is the *only hope of America!* It is <u>why</u> God birthed America!

True Historical Sources:

BOOKS:

The Light and the Glory by Peter Marshall-David Manuel

America's Providential History by Mark Belials-Stephen McDowell

America's God and Country Encyclopedia of Quotations by William Federer

American Dictionary of the English Language (1828 edition) Noah Webster

(All of the above books can presently be ordered from *Christianbook.com* or ordered from your local Christian Bookstore.)

WEBSITES:

www.wallbuilders.com
www.providencefoundation.com
www.plymrock.org
www.amerisearch.net

Endnotes

Chapter 1

[1] Genesis 1: 26-28

[2] See Acts 17:28 "...for in Him we live and move and have our being..."

[3] See 1 Corinthians 6:19

[4] See [Noah] *Webster's 1828 Dictionary of the American Language,* Foundation For American Christian Education, San Francisco, 1967 (reprinted by permission from G. & C. Merriam Co.)

[5] See Genesis 2:9

[6] See John 1:4 "In Him was life and the life was the light of men."

[7] See Genesis 2:9

[8] See *Strong's Exhaustive Concordance,*(James Strong, Madison, N.J., 1890) comment on the word *knowledge* in the reference to Genesis 2:9

Chapter 2

[1] Ephesians 2:4

[2] Dr. Frederick Sampson; heard by the author in the North Carolina Baptist Evangelistic Conference, Ashville, N.C., February, 1976.

[3] See Genesis 18:19

[4] See Deuteronomy 28: 1-14

[5] See Psalm 78-5-6

[6] See Romans 7: 19-23

[7] See Rom. 3:19-20

[8] See Galatians 3:24

Chapter 3

[1] See Luke 1:32

[2] See Matthew 1:21

[3] See 2 Cor. 5:19

[4] See Luke 9:51 & Hebrews 12:2

[5] See John 14:10

[6] See John 11: 49-50

Chapter 4

[1] See John 18:6

[2] See 1 Corinthians 2:8

[3] See Revelation 22:1

[4] See John 19:1-3

[5] Genesis 45: 5-8

[6] See Luke 23:26

[7] See Luke 20:18

[8] See Luke 23:34

[9] See John 19:26-27

[10] See Luke 23:39-43

[11] Luke 23:43

[12] Matthew 27:46

[13] 2 Corinthians 5:21

[14] 1 John 2:2

[15] John 19:28

[16] John 19:30

[17] Colossians 2: 13-15

[18] Luke 23:46

[19] John 19:30

While there are not many details written concerning Jesus' experience in death for three days, we get a faint glimpse of the battle that was waged there (Acts 2:22-32;Col. 2:13-15; 1 Corinthians 2:8; Eph. 1:19-21). We know He was not in His body in the tomb, for death is the separation of the spirit and soul from the body. We know He suffered pain during those three days as recorded in Acts 2;24.

But while there are many things we don't know about those three days he spent in death, the one thing we _do_ know is that the ultimate end was the absolute and total defeat of all the power of death, including the overthrow and "disarming" of our arch enemy, satan! (Col. 2:15)

[20] 2 Corinthians 5:7

[21] John 19:40-42; Luke 23: 50-53

[22] Matthew 27: 62-64

Chapter 5

[1] Luke 8:2

[2] Mt. 28:5-6

[3] Luke. 24:5-7

[4] Mark 16:7

[5] John 20:1-8

[6] John 20:1-18

Chapter 6

[1] Hebrews 12:22-23

[2] Ephesians 4:8-10; (cmpare Ephesians 1:14 "the earnest of our inheritance" or "guarantee" of our inheritance")

[3] Psalms 94:20

[4] Heb. 10:10-14

[5] Hebrews 10: 12

[6] 1 Peter 3:18; 1 Corinthians 1:30

[7] Ephesians 2: 13-18

[8] Rom. 6:6; 2 Cor. 5:21

[9] Romans 6:11

[10] John 8:36

> Note: This isn't to say satan can't work inside us if we live in ignorance of this truth; or if we don't exercise belief in it during a given temptation.

[11] Romans 6:23

[12] Romans 5:12

[13] Heb. 2:14-15

[14] Note the author's comments on pages 3-4 about the reason for which God made man.

[15] 1 Pt. 5:8

[16] Jn. 10:10

[17] Acts 2:24

[18] Hebrews 2:9

[19] John 10:18

[20] 1 John 4:4 (emphasis added)

[21] Hebrews 2:14-15

[22] In Revelation 12:10 satan is called the "Accuser of the brethren."

[23] 1 Corinthians 15:55

[24] Hebrews 2:14-15

[25] Revelation 1:7

Chapter 7

[1] Acts 1:3

[2] Luke 24:13-25

[3] John 20: 26-28

[4] 1 Corinthians 15:6

[5] See *More than a Carpenter*, Josh McDowell, Living Books-Tyndale House, Wheaton, Ill., 1977, pp.52-53.

[6] Acts 1: 6-8

[7] Matthew 28: 18-20

[8] Acts 1: 9-11

Chapter 8

[1] Ez. 36:27 (emphasis added)

[2] Acts 2:1-4

[3] This is what is meant by *repentance*.

[4] Acts 2: 5-41 relates this whole story.

[5] 2 Cor. 6:16

[6] See *America's Providential History,* Belials-McDowell, Providence Press, 1989, p. 37-38.

[7] Matthew 13:24-30

[8] Acts 5:1-11

[9] 2 Corinthians 2: 3-11

[10] 1 Corinthians 12:13, Colossians 1:27, Galatians 2:20, Ephesians 5:30)

Chapter 9

[1] Ezekiel 28: 10-16

While this passage is about the king of Tyre, it is also about the power motivating the king of Tyre, which is satan, himself.

[2] Psalms 23: 4

[3] See Revelation 3:17

Chapter 10

1 *America's Providential History,* p. 43

2 Ibid., p. 43

3 Deuteronomy 1:13 & Exodus 18:21; NASB

4 *Teaching and Learning*, Rosalee Slater, The Foundation for American Christian Education, San Francisco, 1965, p. 166.

5 *America's Providential History, p. 44*

6 Newton, Sir Isaac. 1704, in Optics. John Bartlett, *Bartlett's Familiar Quotations* [Boston: Little, Brown and Company, 1855, 1980], p. 313. (Referenced in *America's God and Country,* W. Federer, Fame Pub. 1994)

7 Jeremiah 29: 13

8 See Hebrews 10:12

9 Luther's counsel upon reading "the twelve articles" of the insurgent peasants of Suabia. as recorded by George Bancroft in his *History of the United States,* Vol. 1 To 1688; Part 1 Chapter 12, *The Pilgrims,* p. 33

Chapter 11

1 *History of the Reformation in Europe in the Time of Calvin,* J. H. Merle D'Aubigne,[Robert Carter and Bros., New York, 1867] as quoted in *Teaching and Learning America's Christian History*, Rosalee Slater, [Foundation for American Christian Education, San Francisco, 1965] p.p. 170-172.

2 *America's Providential History,* p. 48

3 John 3:3

4 1 Corinthians 6:19-20

5 John 1:12, Revelation 3:20

6 Psalms 139:17; 1 Corinthians 2:16

7 *America's Providential History,* p.p. 49-50

8 Early American historians gave witness to the influence of John

Calvin in the shaping of American institutions.

Note the following excerpts from renowned 19th century historian George Bancroft:

"For the regeneration of the world it was requisite that the Divine Being should enter the abodes and hearts of men and dwell there; that a belief in Him should be received which would include all truth respecting His essence; that He should be known, not as a distant Providence of boundless power and uncertain and inactive will, but as God present in the flesh....Amid the deep sorrows of humanity during the sad conflict which was protracted during centuries for the overthrow of the past and the reconstruction of society, the consciousness of an incarnate God carried peace into the bosom of humanity....This doctrine once communicated to man, was not to be eradicated. It spread as widely, as swiftly, and as silently as the light, and the idea of GOD WITH US dwelt and dwells in every system of thought that can pretend to vitality; in every oppressed people, whose struggles to be free have the promise of success; in every soul that sighs for redemption."

(Bancroft, George. In an address entitled, *"The Progress of Mankind." George Bancroft, Literary and Historical Miscellanies*, pp. 502, 504. Stephen Abbot Northrop, D.D., *A Cloud of Witnesses* (Portland, Oregon: American Heritage Ministries, 1987; Mantle Ministries, 228 Still Ridge, Bulverde, Texas), pp. 24-25.)

"At the time of the Revolution, a full two-thirds of the population of America, estimated at 3,000,000 people, had been trained in the teachings of John Calvin: 900,000 were of Scotch or Scotch-Irish origin, 600,000 were Puritan English, 400,000 were German or Dutch Reformed, the Episcopalians had a Calvinistic confession in their Thirty-nine Articles, in addition to the numerous French Huguenots who had come to the western world."

(Bancroft, George. Population of America during Revolutionary period that was indirectly influenced by Reformer John Calvin. Dr. Loraine Boettner, Reformed Doctrine of Predestination (Philadelphia: Presbyterian and Reformed, 1972), p. 382. John Eidsmoe,

Christianity and the Constitution - *The Faith of Our Founding Fathers* (Grand Rapids, MI: Baker Book House, A Mott Media Book, 1987; 6th printing, 1993), p. 19.)

"He who will not honor the memory and respect the influence of Calvin knows little of the origin of American liberty."

(Bancroft, George. Statement regarding the influence on the formation of American institutions by the Reformer John Calvin. Dr. Loraine Boettner, Reformed Doctrine of Predestination (Philadelphia: Presbyterian and Reformed, 1972), pp. 389-90. John Eidsmoe, *Christianity and the Constitution - The Faith of Our Founding Fathers* (Grand Rapids, MI: Baker Book House, A Mott Media Book, 1987; 6th printing, 1993), p. 18.)

[9] Isaiah 9:7

Chapter 12

[1] *Of Plymouth Plantation,* William Bradford, republished by Vision Forum, Bulverde, Texas, in association with *Mantle Ministries,* 1998, p. 6.

[2] *Pilgrim Fathers,* p. 124

[3] The author is chiefly indebted to three volumes which relate the *Pilgrim's* story: *Of Plymouth Plantation,* written by their Governor of 35 years, William Bradford; *The Pilgrim Fathers,* by John Brown; and *The Light and the Glory,* by Peter Marshall, Jr. and David Manuel. These will be duly referenced as they are referred to in this narrative.

[4] *Of Plymouth Plantation,* William Bradford, republished by Vision Forum, Bulverde, Texas, in association with *Mantle Ministries,* 1998, p. 7.

[5] *Ibid.,* p. 124

[6] George Bancroft, *History of the United States,* Vol.1, p.199

[7] *Ibid.* p. 199

[8] George Bancroft, *History of the United States,* Vol.1, p.200 - p.201

[9] Acts 5: 29

[10] Bradford, William. 1607, in his work entitled, *The History of Plymouth Plantation* 1608-1650 (Boston, Massachusetts: Massachusetts Historical Society, 1856; Boston, Massachusetts: Wright and Potter Printing Company, 1898, 1901, from the Original Manuscript, Library of Congress Rare Book Collection, Washington, D.C.; rendered in Modern English, Harold Paget, 1909; NY: Russell and Russell, 1968.

[11] *American Dictionary of the English Language,* Noah Webster, G. & C. Mirriam, 1828; reprinted by permission by Foundation for American Christian Education, San Francisco, 1967.

[12] *Of Plymouth Plantation,* William Bradford, republished by Vision Forum, Bulverde, Texas, in association with *Mantle Ministries,* 1998, p. 13.

[13] As historian George Bancroft would identify the Pilgrim's reason for coming to America: "Conscious of ability to act a higher part in the great drama of humanity, they, after ten years, were moved by "a hope and inward zeal of advancing the gospel of the kingdom of Christ in the remote parts of the New World; yea, though they should be but as stepping-stones unto others for performing so great a work."

(George Bancroft, *History of the United States*, Vol.1, p.201 - p.202)

[14] (From: William Bradford's *Of Plymouth Plantation.* John Robinson's *Farewell Letter* to the Pilgrims, July 1620) Taken from PilgrimHall .org, website, 3/708)

[15] Ibid.

[16] Ibid.

[17] Ibid

[18] Robinson, John. Robert Ashton, ed., *The Works of John Robinson*, Pastor of the Pilgrim Fathers (London: John Snow, 1851), Vol. 2, pp. 140-141.

Chapter 13

1 *Of Plymouth Plantation,* William Bradford, republished by Vision Forum, Bulverde, Texas, in association with *Mantle Ministries,* 1998, p.p. 75-76.

2 No details have ever been found which identify exactly what this "screw" was. Some have suggested it was part of William Brewster's printing press. Others think it was a house jack. The truth is we just don't know exactly what it was. What we do know is that the Pilgrims viewed it as part of God's Providential provision to save them from certain death.

3 The Pilgrims often told this story to their children so they would know it was the *Providence of God* which had brought them safely over "the vast and furious ocean," as Bradford would call it.

The story came to be included in textbooks for school children to read all across America so future generations would know it was the hand of God who had founded this nation. Not until the 1930's, when the humanists came to control our public school systems, did this story start to disappear from the classrooms.

4 *Of Plymouth Plantation,* William Bradford, republished by Vision Forum, Bulverde, Texas, in association with *Mantle Ministries,* 1998, p.p. 75-76.

5 *History of the United States*, George Bancroft, Vol.1, p.208.

6 *Ibid,* p.p. 65-66

7 2 Corinthians 12:9

Chapter 14

1 *Of Plymouth Plantation, p. 21*

2 Inferred from N. Webster's definition of the word *reason* in his 1828 edition of *American Dictionary of the English Language,* [cited above].

³ See 2 Corinthians 3:17

⁴ See 2 Corinthians 5:10

⁵ *Plymouth Plantation, p.* 80

⁶ Ps. 139: 17-18

⁷ *Plymouth Plantation, p. 80*

⁸ *The Pilgrim Fathers*, by John Brown, Pilgrim Publications, Pasadena, Texas, 1970 (reprint of the 1890's edition), p. 220.

⁹ Matthew 5:42

¹⁰ Jackson, Andrew. June 8, 1845. Henry Halley, *Halley's Bible Handbook* (Grand Rapids, MI: Zondervan, 1927, 1965), p. 18. Stephen McDowell and Mark Beliles, "The Providential Perspective" (Charlottesville, VA: The Providence Foundation, P.O. Box 6759, Charlottesville, Va. 22906, January 1994), Vol. 9, No. 1, p. 6.

¹¹ *Of Plymouth Plantation, p.6*

¹² See 2 Corinthians 5:18-19

¹³ See John 1:12; Colossians 1:27

¹⁴ Mark 1:14-15

¹⁵ Though taught by their words and seen by their actions in their history, one of the greatest statements identifying this is to be found in Daniel Webster's statement as footnoted on p. 148. Webster, Daniel, The Works of D. Webster (Boston, Little, Brown and Co., 1853) Vol. I, p. 48

Chapter 15

¹ Hancock, John. 1774. George Bancroft, *History of the United States of America*, 6 vols. (Boston: Charles C. Little and James Brown, Third Edition, 1838), Vol. II, p. 229. Lucille Johnston, *Celebrations of a Nation* (Arlington, VA: The Year of Thanksgiving Foundation, 1987), p. 77. Peter Marshall and David Manuel, *The Light and the Glory* (Old Tappan, New Jersey: Fleming H. Revell Co., 1977), p. 269.

[2] *John Adams and the American Revolution,* Catherine Bowen, Little Brown and Co., Boston, 1950, p. 583

[3] Adams, John. July 1, 1776, in speaking to the delegates of the Continental Congress. Daniel Webster, "Speech of John Adams," William H. McGuffey, *McGuffey's Eclectic Fifth Reader* (Cincinnati and New York: Van Antwerp, Bragg & Co., revised edition, 1879; NY: American Book Company, 1907; revised 1920), lesson LXVI, p. 199. D.P. Diffine, Ph.D., *One Nation Under God - How Close a Separation?* (Searcy, Arkansas: Harding University, Belden Center for Private Enterprise Education, 6th edition, 1992), p. 7.

[4] Henry, Patrick. March 23, 1775, in The Second Virginia Convention given at St. John's Church in Richmond Virginia. *The Annals of America*, 20 vols. (Chicago, IL: Encyclopedia Britannica,) George Bancroft, *History of the United States of America*, 6 vols. (Boston: Charles C. Little and James Brown, Third Edition, 1838), p. 29. Peter Marshall and David Manual, *The Light and the Glory* (Old Tappan, NJ: Fleming Revell Co., 1977), p. 269.

[5] *Christianity and the Constitution,* John Eidsmoe, Baker Book House, Grand Rapids, MI, 1987, p. 81

[6] Witherspoon, John. Edward Frank Humphrey, *Nationalism and Religion* (Boston: Chipman Law Publishing Co., 1924), p. 85. Peter Marshall and David Manuel, *The Glory of America* (Bloomington, MN: Garborg's Heart'N Home, Inc., 1991), 2.5.

[7] Washington, George. July 20, 1788, in a letter written from Mount Vernon to the Governor of Connecticut, Jonathan Trumbull. Jared Sparks, ed., *The Writings of George Washington* 12 vols. (Boston: American Stationer's Company, 1837; NY: F. Andrew's, 1834-1847), Vol. IX, p. 397. Peter Marshall and David Manuel, *The Glory of America* (Bloomington, MN: Garborg's Heart'N Home, Inc., 1991), 7.20.

[8] Madison, James. 1815, in a Presidential Proclamation. James D. Richardson (U.S. Representative from Tennessee), ed., *A Compilation of the Messages and Papers of the Presidents 1789-1897*, 10 vols. (Washington, D.C.: U.S. Government Printing Office, published by Authority of Congress, 1897, 1899; Washington, D.C.: Bureau of National Literature and Art, 1789-1902, 11 vols., 1907, 1910). Benjamin Franklin Morris, *The Christian Life and Character of the Civil Institutions of the United States* (Philadelphia: George W. Childs, 1864), p. 550.

[9] 2 Timothy 2:21

Epilogue

[1] (1766. Webster, Daniel. *The Works of Daniel Webster* (Boston: Little, Brown and Company, 1853), Vol. I, p. 48. "Our Christian Heritage," Letter from Plymouth Rock (Marlborough, NH: The Plymouth Rock Foundation), p. 5. Peter Marshall and David Manuel, *The Glory of America* (Bloomington, MN: Garborg's Heart'N Home, Inc., 1991), 12.22. Marshall Foster and Mary-Elaine Swanson, *The American Covenant - The Untold Story* (Roseburg, OR: Foundation for Christian Self-Government, 1981; Thousand Oaks, CA: The Mayflower Institute, 1983, 1992), p. 158.

[2] 1495. *Webster, Noah. 1832. History of the United States* (New Haven: Durrie & Peck, 1832), pp. 273-274, 300, paragraph 578. Verna M. Hall, *The Christian History of the American Revolution* (San Francisco: Foundation for American Christian Education, 1976), p. 255. Peter Marshall and David Manuel, *The Glory of America* (Bloomington, Garborg's Heart'N Home, Inc., 1991), 1.22.

[3] 126 Adams, John Quincy. July 4, 1821. John Wingate Thornton, *The Pulpit of the American Revolution 1860* (reprinted NY: Burt Franklin, 1860; 1970), p. XXIX. Verna M. Hall, comp., Christian History of the Constitution of the United States of

America (San Francisco: Foundation for American Christian Education, 1976), p. 372. Marshall Foster and Mary-Elaine Swanson, *The American Covenant - The Untold Story* (Roseburg, OR: Foundation for Christian Self-Government, 1981; Thousand Oaks, CA: The Mayflower Institute, 1983, 1992), p. 18.

[4] Adams, John. February 1765, in his notes for A Dissertation on the Canon and Feudal Law. Benjamin Franklin Morris, *The Christian Life and Character of the Civil Institutions of the United States* (Philadelphia: George W. Childs, 1864), p. 109. John Eidsmoe, *Christianity and the Constitution - The Faith of Our Founding Fathers* (Grand Rapids, MI: Baker Book House, A Mott Media Book, 1987; 6th printing, 1993), p. 266. Peter Marshall and David Manuel, *The Glory of America* (Bloomington, MN: Garborg's Heart'N Home, Inc., 1991), 2.1.

[5] *The Power of Prayer,* by R.A. Torrey, Fleming H. Revell, 1924, p. 1 of the Introduction.

[6] Franklin, Benjamin. 1739. Benjamin Franklin, *The Autobiography of Benjamin Franklin* (New York: Books,Inc., 1791), p. 146.

Benjamin Franklin, Autobiography, 1771-75 (Reprinted Garden City, NY: Garden City Publishing Co., Inc., 1916),Vol. 1, pp. 191-192. John Pollack, *George Whitefield and the Great Awakening* (Garden City New Jersey: Doubleday and Co., 1972), p. 117. John Eidsmoe, *Christianity and The Constitution - The Faith of Our Founding Fathers* (Grand Rapids, MI: Baker Book House, 1987), p. 204.

[7] *(Christianity & the Constitution,* J. Eidsmoe p.58

[8] *Finney Lives On,* by V Raymond Edman, Bethany Fellowship Press, Minneapolis, 1951, p.68

[9] See Hebrews 13:8

[10] Genesis 1:26

[11] John 8:32

[12] 1 John 1:9

[13] Proverbs 28:13

[14] Romans 12:1-2

[15] *America's Providential History,* p.186

[16] Marshall, Peter. 1947, in a message as Chaplain of the United States Senate. Robert Flood, *The Rebirth of America* (Philadelphia: Arthur S. DeMoss Foundation, 1986), p. 205. Peter Marshall and David Manuel, *The Glory of America* (Bloomington, MN: Garborg's Heart 'N Home, Inc., 1991), 1.13.

[17] (2296. Lincoln, Abraham. March 30, 1863, in a Proclamation of a National Day of Humiliation, Fasting and Prayer. James D. Richardson (U.S. Representative from Tennessee), ed., *A Compilation of the Messages and Papers of the Presidents 1789-1897,* 10 vols. (Washington, D.C.: U.S. Government Printing Office, published by Authority of Congress, 1897, 1899; Washington, D.C.: Bureau of National Literature and Art, 1789-1902, 11 vols., 1907, 1910), Vol. VI, pp. 164-165. Gary DeMar, *America's Christian History: The Untold Story* (Atlanta, GA: American Vision Publishers, Inc., 1993), pp. 53, 99.)

[18] (2297. Lincoln, Abraham. June 1863, in a discourse with a college President, just weeks before the Battle of Gettysburg, July 1-3, 1863. William J. Johnson, Abraham Lincoln, The Christian (NY: The Abington Press, 1913), pp. 109-110. Peter Marshall and David Manuel, The Glory of America (Bloomington, MN: Garborg's Heart 'N Home, Inc., 1991), 4.26.)

[19] (Stowe, Harriet Beecher. 1852. Harriet Beecher Stowe, Uncle Tom's Cabin (1852), p. 458. Peter Marshall and David Manuel, The Glory of America (Bloomington, MN: Garborg's Heart 'N Home, Inc., 1991), 3.20.)

[20] Galatians 2:20